Vardis Fisher's Boise

Written for the Federal Writers' Project

Introduction by
Alessandro Meregaglia

Copyright © 2019 by Rediscovered Publishing
All rights reserved. This book or any portion thereof may not be reproduced or used in any manner whatsoever without the express written permission of the publisher except for the use of brief quotations in a book review.

Printed in the United States of America

Author: Vardis Fisher
Editors: Laura Wally Johnston & Alessandro Meregaglia
Cover design: Ward Hooper
Interior layout and design: Jane Alice Van Doren

The Boise Guide was compiled by the Federal Writers' Project of the Works Progrss Administration, 1939

First Printing, 2019

ISBN: 978-0-9988909-8-2

Rediscovered Publishing
180 N 8th Street
Boise, Idaho 83712

www.rediscoveredpublishing.com

Table of Contents

Vardis Fisher and the Boise Guide: A Brief History..................7

    The Bad Boy of Idaho: Vardis Fisher and the Federal Writers' Project..........9

    Writing The Boise Guide..................13

    Discovering the Forgotten Fisher Manuscript..................21

    Commentary About the Guide..................26

Editors' Note..................32

The Boise Guide..................35

Introduction..................36

    Information for Tourists..................37

    Calendar of Events..................43

    Statistical Review..................45

Part I: Boise Today..................51

    Physical Aspect..................51

    The Streets..................54

    Natural Setting..................59

    Racial Elements..................64

    The Press..................69

    Radio..................76

    Industries...78
    Churches...81
    Schools..87
    The Arts...95
    Parks and Playgrounds..101

Part II: Chronology (prepared with Milton Mills)....................105

    Prehistory...105
    1805-1937..106

Part III: Points of Interest..177

    The State Capitol..177
    Union Pacific Station..181
    Julia Davis Park...183
    O'Farrell Cabin..186
    DeLamar House..187
    Bohemian Breweries...189

Part IV: Tours in Environs...193

    Tour I: Boise to Table Rock and Return...................................193
    Tour II: Boise, Arrowrock Dam, Atlanta, and Return.......................196

Acknowledgements........................201

Vardis Fisher's Boise
Written for the Federal Writers' Project

By Vardis Fisher

Introduced and Transcribed by
Alessandro Meregaglia

Edited by
Laura Wally Johnston and Alessandro Meregaglia

Rediscovered Publishing

6

Vardis Fisher & The Boise Guide

A Brief History

By Alessandro Meregaglia

Vardis Fisher (Vardis and Opal Fisher Papers. Courtesy of Boise State Special Collections and Archives)

The Bad Boy of Idaho: Vardis Fisher and the Federal Writers' Project

The *Boise Guide* sat in a box in Washington, D.C. untouched for nearly 80 years. It was a product of the Federal Writers' Project (FWP), a federal government program and division of the Works Progress Administration (WPA) intended to provide jobs for unemployed writers during the Great Depression. Although the FWP was centralized in Washington, D.C., each state had its own director and staff who were responsible for producing work. In Idaho, the Writers' Project created three published books: *Idaho: A Guide in Word and Picture* (1937), *The Idaho Encyclopedia* (1938), and *Idaho Lore* (1939), a sizeable output for a small state.[1]

The person almost single-handedly responsible for the success of the Writers' Project in Idaho was Vardis Fisher. A novelist and writer born in eastern Idaho, Fisher was appointed the first director of the Idaho Writers' Project in October 1935. At the time of his appointment, Fisher had already published a book of poetry and five novels as well as a collection of essays. (He would go on to write thirty more books in his long career.)

1. Idaho technically also produced *Tours in Eastern Idaho* (1937), a small pamphlet that consisted of driving tours excerpted from the larger *Idaho Guide*.

The first task given to Fisher (and to all states) was to produce a guide book covering the entire state for the American Guide Series, billed as "a guide to the progress of American civilization."[2] The book was to include driving tours for the entire state, a brief history, and descriptive information about the area's natural and cultural resources. Fisher had great difficulty getting a staff together because, as he said, "Idaho is not, of course, a state of unemployed writers."[3] He also faced unsupportive Idaho WPA staff: when Fisher reported to work in Pocatello, near his home, they had no interest in assisting him and initially gave him no office space. Since that arrangement was unsuitable, he moved the Idaho Writers' Project offices to Boise, where they remained during his tenure. But Fisher didn't let that set him back, and he immediately got to work on the state guide.

Working almost entirely by himself, Fisher moved quickly on the manuscript and finished the whole copy in less than a year—far faster than the federal office anticipated—and was ready to publish it in fall 1936. His close friendship with James H. Gipson, owner of Caxton Printers, contributed to this speed. Caxton, a book publisher located in Caldwell, Idaho, had previously published Fisher's novels and was willing to prioritize the *Idaho Guide* in their printing schedule.[4]

2. Publicity Materials, "The American Guide," Box 1, Entry 12, PI-57, RG 69, National Archives at College Park.

3. Vardis Fisher to Henry Alsberg, August 15, 1936, "Idaho," Box 11, Entry 1, PI-57, RG 69, National Archives at College Park.

4. Caxton also assumed all of the risk because the sponsoring agencies did not subsidize the publishing.

J. H. Gipson and Vardis Fisher stand outside the Caxton offices (Vardis and Opal Fisher Papers. Courtesy of Boise State Special Collections and Archives)

The Washington, D.C. office, especially Henry Alsberg, the national director of the FWP, made every effort to stall publication; they wanted the Washington, D.C. guide book published first. Alsberg tried bogging Fisher down by asking for over two thousand revisions to the manuscript. Alsberg then tried sending assistant project director George Cronyn to Idaho to intimidate Fisher. But Fisher, with Gipson's help, "got him drunk, and ... put him on the train and sent him back to Washington, and we went ahead and published the guide."[5] Thus Fisher succeeded in the end. *Idaho: A Guide in Word and Picture* was the first guide book published by the Writers Project. Even thirty years later, Fisher still took delight in his success at getting the *Idaho Guide* out first: the "bureaucratic bastards in Washington tried to stop me from publishing it, lest it 'embarrass' the other states! I got it published in spite of all their roadblocks and it embarrassed them plenty!"[6]

Despite how much trouble Fisher had with the national office, the *Guide* was a success: the reviews were excellent; the entire country took notice of Idaho, Fisher, and the FWP, especially since the project finally had something to show for all of its expenditures. Because of the positive attention his book brought to the entire Writers' Project, Fisher managed to maintain a working relationship with the

5. Vardis Fisher interview with John Milton, South Dakota Public Television, March 20, 1967. Typed transcript found in the Idaho State Archives Oral History Collection, OH 1030.

6. Fisher to Monty Penkower, June 20, 1967, Folder 7, Box 1, Cage 229, Vardis Fisher Papers, Manuscripts, Archives, and Special Collections, Washington State University Libraries.

national office. Alsberg even referred to him as "the bad boy of the Project."[7]

Writing *The Boise Guide*

Early on in the preparation of the state guide, the Washington office suggested to Fisher that Idaho produce city guides for Boise and Pocatello "providing that there would seem to be some advantage so far as gaining local support in those two cities."[8] (Pocatello was the second largest city in Idaho at the time.) From that statement, it appears that the purpose of the local guides was less for tourism and more to encourage support of the WPA's programs. Fisher, however, initially dismissed that idea—"a city guide of Boise would be ridiculous"—because he thought the city wasn't large enough or with enough unique qualities.[9] A few months later, he reiterated that "there is no necessity for the publication of city Guides or even of local Guides, so nothing has been done in that respect."[10]

Fisher instead focused on publishing the statewide *Idaho Guide*, which happened in January 1937. He immediately shifted his energy to the *Idaho Encyclopedia*, which became the first and only statewide encyclopedia for the FWP.

7. Jerre Mangione, *The Dream and the Deal: The Federal Writers' Project, 1935-1943* (Boston: Little, Brown, and Co., 1972), 208.

8. George W. Cronyn to Fisher, December 5, 1935, "Idaho State Guide: Miscellaneous," Box 11, Entry 13, PI-57, RG 69, National Archives at College Park.

9. Fisher to Cronyn, April 11, 1936, "Idaho State Guide: Miscellaneous," Box 11, Entry 13, PI-57, RG 69, National Archives at College Park.

10. Fisher to Alsberg, August 21, 1936, "Idaho," Box 11, Entry 1, PI-57, RG 69, National Archives at College Park.

At some point in mid-1937, with work on the encyclopedia well under way, Fisher turned his attention to several new projects: a book about Idaho folklore, one about all the recreational areas in Idaho (titled early on as "Idaho Playgrounds"), and a city guide about Boise. Only the first one came to fruition, as *Idaho Lore* in 1939.

It's not clear what prompted Fisher's change of mind and led him to begin researching and writing the *Boise Guide*. Whatever the reason, though, the project was doomed from the start: Fisher could find no one to sponsor the *Guide*. Sponsorship was requisite for anything published through the FWP, since sponsors helped circumvent a federal law that requires anything produced by a federal agency to be published by the Government Printing Office.[11] The other task was to secure a publisher to actually produce the book. J. H. Gipson of Caxton Printers was again willing to have his company publish Fisher's work and even risk financial loss, since he thought it was a worthwhile project.[12]

Just a few months after starting work on the *Guide*, Fisher already started to worry about the *Guide*'s viability. "The Mayor and the City Council of Boise refuse to sponsor the volume I take it, because they are all republicans. Inasmuch as the sale

11. Regulations for Publication of State and Local Guide Material, August 10, 1937, "Miscellaneous Folder #3," Box 1, Entry 2, PI-57, RG 69, National Archives at College Park.

12. James H. Gipson to Fisher, December 23, 1937, Folder 30, Box 12, Cage 873, The Caxton Printers, Ltd. Records, 1928-1982, Manuscripts, Archives, and Special Collections, Washington State University Libraries.

Vardis Fisher at Caxton Printers, 1939 (Vardis and Opal Fisher Papers. Courtesy of Boise State Special Collections and Archives)

on this book will be very small, it looks as if we are going to have difficulty in getting it out," he wrote to the federal office.¹³

Two months later, in September 1938, Fisher wrote to Alsberg explaining the great difficulty he continued to have finding a sponsor for the *Boise Guide*. "The chamber of commerce and city council are made up of fine republican gents for whom everything WPA

13. Fisher to Alsberg, July 6, 1938, "Idaho: Boise Guide," Box 11, Entry 13, PI-57, RG 69, National Archives at College Park.

stinks to the high heavens," he wrote. The Idaho State Historical Society, apparently, was only willing to sponsor statewide publications and not local content. The State Library, too, was equally unwilling because, according to Fisher, "the board is composed of old reactionaries who would not even listen to the proposal, much less accept it." The editors of Boise's newspapers, though both Republicans, were willing to support it editorially, but a government agency or non-profit had to be the one to sponsor it.[14]

Those against the *Guide* were opposed more generally to the WPA and the enormous amount of money the agency was spending. A newspaper article quoted the secretary of the Boise Merchants' Bureau suggesting the project was getting out of scope in response to Fisher's pitch to the Chamber of Commerce requesting support for the *Guide*: "The writers' project is going far afield. The WPA is not in the selling business." [15]

Gipson nonetheless was fully supportive of the *Boise Guide*. He discussed with Fisher how best to advertise the booklet and also the logistics of printing it, too. He committed his firm to a sixty-day turnaround time to print the *Guide* once the manuscript was approved and even pushed ahead with advertising the book.[16]

14. Fisher to Alsberg, September 7, 1938, "Idaho: Boise Guide," Box 11, Entry 13, PI-57, RG 69, National Archives at College Park.

15. "Merchants Rap Tourist Book," *Idaho Statesman*, August 27, 1938, 10.

16. Gipson to Fisher, December 23, 1937, Folder 30, Box 12, Cage 873, The Caxton Printers, Ltd. Records, 1928-1982, Manuscripts, Archives, and Special Collections, Washington State University Libraries.

By the end of 1937, Caxton still had a large quantity of the *Idaho Guide* in stock. Up to that point, they had lost money publishing it. To try to sell off the remaining books, Caxton worked with Fisher

> SPONSORSHIP FOR BOISE GUIDE
>
> Dear Mr. Alsberg:
>
> I am still unable to find a sponsor for the Boise guide. The chamber of commerce and city council are made up of fine republican gents for whom everything WPA stinks to the high heavens. State Historical Society does not feel it should sponsor anything but Statewide publications. You suggested I try the library; but there again the board is composed of old reactionaries who would not even listen to the proposal, much less accept it. I'm trying to get the Secretary of State to sponsor it but he balks because he does not happen to vote in this county. He lost by 200 votes the nomination to replace D. Worth Clark who replaces Pope----and perhaps that disappointment has soured him a bit.
>
> Months ago Gipson of the Caxton Printers persuaded me to go ahead and complete this guide; and said he'd try to assist in finding a sponsor here. The editors of both local papers, one a Republican, have promised to go to bat for it in their editorial columns----but I don't want to start a controversy.
>
> In such difficult cases, have you in any other cities taken care of the matter of sponsorship in some other way? Do you have any further suggestions?
>
> Yours very truly,
>
> Vardis Fisher, Director
> Idaho Writers' Project

Vardis Fisher to Henry Alsberg, September 7, 1938 (Courtesy of the National Archives)

and Alsberg in the national office to send around a circular advertisement listing all the Idaho FWP books both published and forthcoming. This circular was

17. Draft of Circular Advertisement, January 12, 1938, "Idaho Encyclopedia," Box 11, Entry 13, PI-57, RG 69, National Archives at College Park.

18. Caxton Trade List 1939-40, "Caxton Printers," Box 54, Wendell Holmes Stephenson Papers, David M. Rubenstein Rare Book & Manuscript Library, Duke University.

19. Gipson to Fisher, December 27, 1937, Folder 30, Box 12, Cage 873, The Caxton Printers, Ltd. Records, 1928-1982, Manuscripts, Archives, and Special Collections, Washington State University Libraries.

20. Fisher to Alsberg, December 27, 1937, "Idaho: Boise Guide," Box 11, Entry 13, PI-57, RG 69, National Archives at College Park.

Opposite Page: Vardis Fisher at his desk, 1939 (Vardis and Opal Fisher Papers. Courtesy of Boise State Special Collections and Archives)

ultimately sent to 50,000 people and contributed greatly to selling the remaining 3,000 volumes. And it contained the first announcement of the new *Boise Guide*: "This guide to Idaho's capital and largest city will be available April 20, 1938 [wishful thinking]. It will be a small cloth-bound attractive book, lavishly illustrated, and will probably sell for $1.25."[17]

Caxton continued to anticipate the publication of the *Boise Guide* and listed it in their 1939-40 Trade List with a "date to be determined."[18] Despite the advertising, Gipson admitted he didn't "see a large sale for the *Boise Guide*" and hoped for a sale of 500 copies in the first year.[19]

Gipson and Fisher also discussed the physical format of the book. Gipson preferred a cloth-bound book with approximately 60 pages of text and 50-60 photographs, and a few maps.[20] Fisher concurred and wrote to the national office that the volume would be "sixty to seventy pages, lavishly illustrated, the whole job lithographed, to sell for not more than a dollar."[21]

Fisher continued to make progress on the *Guide* throughout 1938, but "digging out Boise history accurately has turned out to be a most difficult job."[22] He finally sent in his draft of the *Boise Guide* in late

November 1938 to the Washington FWP office for approval, but left out "maps, photographs, and a few drawings."[23] For the next twelve months, Fisher made no progress on securing a sponsor. To their credit, Alsberg continued to check in with Fisher about the *Boise Guide*; the FWP appeared anxious to issue it.[24] But Fisher's final comment about the *Guide* suggests he had given up: "I have no assurance yet we can get sponsorship for the *Boise Guide* in this provincial and reactionary town."[25] Fisher turned his attention to other projects instead.

21. Fisher to Gipson, December 22, 1937, Folder 30, Box 12, Cage 873, The Caxton Printers, Ltd. Records, 1928-1982, Manuscripts, Archives, and Special Collections, Washington State University Libraries.

22. Fisher to Alsberg, July 15, 1938, "Idaho: Boise Guide," Box 11, Entry 13, PI-57, RG 69, National Archives at College Park.

23. Fisher to Alsberg, November 29, 1938, "Idaho 651.3172 Local Guides," Box 1175, Central Files: State, 1935-1944, RG 69, National Archives at College Park.

24. Alsberg to Fisher, March 16, 1939, "Idaho: Editorial Miscellaneous," Box 11, Entry 13, PI-57, RG 69, National Archives at College Park.

25. Fisher to Alsberg, March 18, [1939], "Vardis Fisher," Box 30, Entry 13, PI-57, RG 69, National Archives at College Park.

26. Fisher was fed up with the Washington bureaucracy and interested in devoting more of his time to his own writing. He had published *Children of God* earlier that year, which was his most well-reviewed novel and earned him the Harper Prize. Florence Kerr to O. K. Hine, October 18, 1939, "Idaho 651.3171," Box 1175, Central Files: State, 1935-1944, RG 69, National Archives at College Park.

27. "Vardis Fisher Expresses His Viewpoint," *Lincoln County Journal*, 1965. [Exact date unknown.] Folder 6, Box 1, Cage 229, Vardis Fisher Papers, Manuscripts, Archives, and Special Collections, Washington State University Libraries.

28. Fisher to Alsberg, November 1, 1936, "Idaho," Box 11, Entry 1, PI-57, RG 69, National Archives at College Park.

Then, for unrelated reasons, Fisher resigned the Writers' Project on November 7, 1939.[26] In a somewhat paranoid fashion, Fisher claimed that there were "spies" monitoring his moves and reporting on him to the Idaho WPA office.[27] This came as little surprise since Fisher had threatened to quit three years earlier during the fiasco getting out the state guide.[28] It appears Fisher's primary reason for leaving, though, was to pursue fiction-writing full time.[29]

> You have the power and we are holding the sack. If you choose to make this a give and take matter, if you will be reasonable and especially in matters in which you are now obviously unreasonable, and if you will not force us to include in this library edition a lot of material that we don't want, then we can go ahead. If you will not, then we have only two possible courses left to us. We shall indefinitely postpone the book until such time as you are willing to be reasonable——and I imagine that time will come after you learn, six months or a year from now, that some of the states will not be able to publish their guides even if you give them carte blanche. Or I can recognize that you have put me on the spot with the Caxton Printers, can reimburse them for their loss out of my own pocket, and send you my resignation.
>
> Yours truly,
>
> Vardis Fisher, Director
> Idaho Writers' Project

The manuscript for the *Boise Guide* was not returned to Boise until January 17, 1940— a full fourteen months after Fisher submitted it. By way of explanation for the delay, the Washington office simply wrote "the manuscript was misplaced."[30] By that time, however, the Writers' Project in Idaho was almost defunct; it shut down on March 20, 1940.

Flora E. Foster, the appointed director after Fisher resigned, expressed sadness about the unpublished manuscripts.[31] When the Idaho Writers' Project did shut down, it appears that the manuscripts were sent back to the D.C. office, filed away in a box, and forgotten about for almost eighty years.

Discovering the Forgotten Fisher Manuscript

If it weren't for a few clues that hinted at its existence, the manuscript may have stayed hidden in a box for eighty more years. Requiring an archival expedition, the path that led to the manuscript's discovery started with my research into Caxton Printers. As an archivist at Boise State University, I was intrigued by Caxton's history as a publisher in the West who competed successfully against Eastern publishers. Through my research, I looked into Caxton's involvement with Fisher and all of the published Federal Writers' Project books.

Reading about the history of the *Idaho Guide* in Jerre Mangione's *The Dream and the Deal*, I first learned about unpublished manuscripts produced by the FWP. There, on page 370, was a footnote with

29. Vardis Fisher, "Vardis Fisher Is Taking to the Hills: Quitting Boise to Write Another Novel," Idaho Statesman, November 7, 1939, 1.

Opposite Page: The concluding paragraph of Fisher's scathing six-page letter to the federal office expressing his frustration with their behavior publishing the *Idaho Guide*, November 1, 1936. (Courtesy of the National Archives)

30. C. E. Triggs to Dean W. Miller, January 17, 1940, "Idaho 651.3172 Local Guides," Box 1175, Central Files: State, 1935-1944, RG 69, National Archives at College Park.

31. Foster to J. D. Newsom, March 12, 1940, "Idaho 651.3173," Box 1175, Central Files: State, 1935-1944, RG 69, National Archives at College Park.

privately owned. In 1864 it was announced in the *Statesman* by one of these enterprising pedagogues that he could teach anyone penmanship so flawless that correspondents would not go crazy trying to decipher epistles from Boise. By 1865 the *Statesman's* editor was campaigning for a public school system but persons gave no heed except to study his diction and rhetoric.

The Territorial legislatures did nothing to help. ~~They kicked the public school bills around until they wore them out or lost them.~~ The tax of one percent to support schools was collected by the sheriff and he retained six-tenths of it as his commission. Even at that, he did not become wealthy. The legislature in 1881 created the Boise Independent School District. Thereupon a board was elected, ~~and~~ an ornate building ~~set up to the disgust and dismay of a considerable number of tax-payers.~~ *erected* and A graduate of Bates College in Maine was invited to become superintendent; *which* and he did with such lusty regard for sound applications of the hickory stick that he was forced to resign. It was foolishness, in the first place, to want to educate the sons and daughters of parents who had done very well without education; and it was downright folly to try to flog them into learning. Nevertheless the American craze for education, by this time a world phenomenon, had its way and the tax-payers had to yield.

Whittier school was completed in 1894, a homely red brick unit of four rooms. In 1898 a second story was added, and today the building stands at Twelfth and Fort Streets, one of the historic landmarks of the city. In 1917 the roof was burned off and since then the building has suffered neglect. A survey of Boise schools in 1920 declared the building to be unsanitary and the grounds insufficient, but it held its own until 1936 when it was taken over by a division of the Works Progress Administration. Today, serious adults ponder the inscrutable problems of the world where thirty years ago unruly youngsters spent most of their time plotting new ways to flabbergast their teachers.

Two years after the Whittier was built the district was again overcrowded; and as a consequence the Lincoln school was built at Fourth and Idaho. ~~It has a facade of mixed parentage, topped by pineapple spires.~~ A Caldwell contractor by name of Miller agreed to erect it for $15,000 but went broke and fled, leaving his bondsmen to finish the job. Today, Lincoln is the district's 'opportunity' school for pupils who need

— *What about the old Central school? RT.*

Original *Boise Guide* typescript with editorial notes from the national office.

a revealing quotation from Vardis Fisher: "At the time of my resignation, I had three more books in manuscript, two large and one small . . . I have no idea where these manuscripts are— buried somewhere, I assume, under the monstrous bureaucracy in Washington."[32]

It was from that small footnote that I managed eventually to track down the *Boise Guide*.[33] Intrigued by these unpublished manuscripts and hoping they had been saved, I looked into Mangione's papers, which are located at the University of Rochester, to get more information. I requested copies of Mangione's and Fisher's correspondence as well as the tapes of their interview. In the interview I heard Fisher say he had written a guide to Boise. Knowing that there had at one point been a manuscript propelled me further. I learned that the Library of Congress possessed a huge collection of WPA records,

CONTAINER	CONTENTS
	Federal Writers' Project: American Guide File, 1524-1941 (continued)
	Local Guide File, 1938-1941 (continued)
	"Seeing Fernandina"
BOX A562	Tampa
	(2 folders)
	Idaho, Boise
	Indiana
	Madison County
	Morgan County
	Vanderburgh County

32. Mangione, *The Dream and the Deal*, 370.

33. There are, in fact, four additional unpublished manuscripts: *Idaho Digest for Travelers, Origins of Idaho Place Names, Idaho Plants and Animals,* and *Idaho Miscellany*. Archival correspondence indicates that Flora Foster wrote most of *Idaho Plants and Animals*. (Foster to J. D. Newsom, March 12, 1940, "Idaho 651.3173," Box 1175, Central Files: State, 1935-1944, RG 69, National Archives at College Park.) Equivalent material from the place names volume later appeared in *Idaho Place Names: A Geographical Dictionary* by Lalia Phipps Boone (1988). The idea for Idaho Miscellany was to compile previously uncollected stories and information about the state; it's by no means a finished manuscript but instead a large amount of unsorted material.

The original cover design for The Boise Guide by William Runyan (Vardis Fisher Papers. Courtesy of Beinecke Library)

but I knew that the National Archives and Records Administration had WPA records as well. I found the inventory for the WPA Records housed at the Library of Congress. There, tucked between folders for Florida and Indiana, was the only digital record of the *Boise Guide* manuscript.[34]

In August 2018, I traveled to Washington, D.C. to consult the collection. To my great delight, Box A562 did indeed contain the manuscript for Fisher's *Boise Guide*. In fact, it contained two copies: one was a carbon copy that Fisher must have kept in his office in Idaho, and the other was the copy with editorial comments from the national office (that wasn't returned until 1940 and then was obviously sent back to D.C.). The edits from the federal office slashed straight through Fisher's voice. In many ways, it's fortuitous that the *Guide* was never published. Had the edits been adopted (as they most surely would have if a sponsor had ever been secured, since Fisher was no longer attached to the Idaho Writers' Project and could register no objection), they would have rendered the *Guide* useful but unimaginative.

In 1942, essayist and historian Bernard DeVoto wrote about the importance of "the enormous mass of data" the FWP gathered. He worried these unpublished manuscripts would be destroyed as "waste paper" but noted that if the documents were "organized, indexed, and made available to . . . historians they can be immensely valuable."[35] The success of not only finding Fisher's manuscript but bringing

34. United States Work Projects Administration records, 1524-1975, MSS 55715, Library of Congress Manuscript Division. https://lccn.loc.gov/mm82055715.

35. Bernard DeVoto, "The Writers' Project," *Harper's Magazine* 184 (January 1942), 220.

it out in print illustrates DeVoto's claim about the importance of the WPA records. The history of the *Boise Guide* is drawn from correspondence found in the National Archives in Washington, D.C., which holds most of the correspondence for the Federal Writers' Project not held by the Library of Congress. The original cover for this *Guide*, drawn by William Runyan, was discovered in Fisher's papers held by Yale University's Beinecke Library.

Commentary About the Guide

The *Boise Guide* reflects Fisher's usual tone and style: direct, at times witty, and almost always acerbic. He is no simple booster or economic promoter; he will only deign to comment on places and things of genuine note. As Fisher makes clear in the Introduction to *Idaho Digest for Travelers* (one of his other unpublished FWP manuscripts), "In the following list only those points of interest are given which it is felt are worthy of attention. If such items as the universities and other institutions or public buildings such as the State Capitol are omitted, it is because they are unimpressive in comparison with corresponding features in many other states." [36]

Fisher strictly limited his scope to the Boise city limits of 1938. He made no mention of Ustick

36. "Idaho Digest for Travelers," Box A783, WPA Records, Library of Congress Manuscript Division.

or Barber Valley, for example. He also avoided any distinctions between neighborhoods or platted additions, which is notable in contrast to today's local

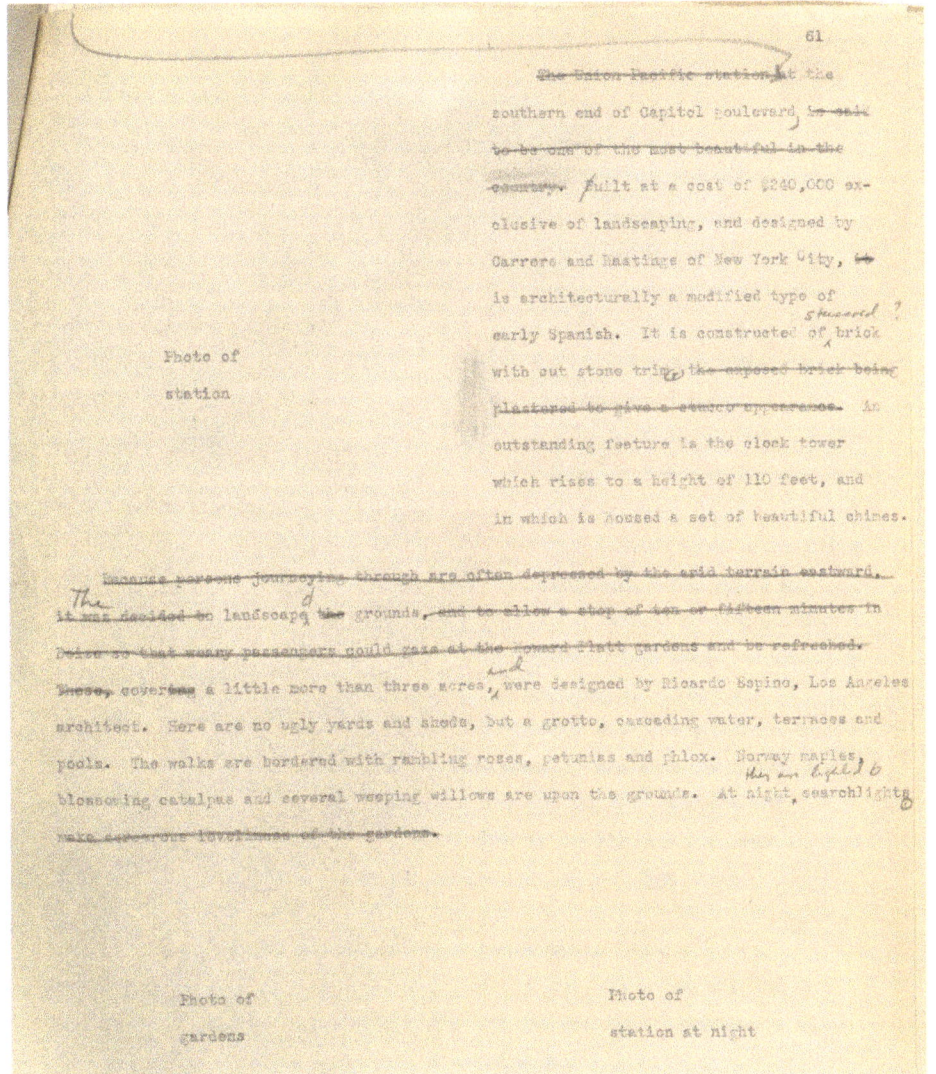

Original *Boise Guide* typescript with editorial notes from the national office.

histories. Because the *Guide* is part tourbook and part history, it's fascinating to see how elements of the city's past were told then versus how they're understood now. The *Guide* also hints at topics that can be explored further by today's historians, such as the fights over getting the elementary school buildings built.

In addition to Fisher's principle of selection for what he included, Fisher also inserted his own commentary, much to the consternation of the Washington office, who instructed Fisher that "personal opinions and derogatory remarks must be deleted."[37] Fisher ignored that request. And that makes the manuscript all the more interesting. The editorial report noted there is "a type of flippant writing" throughout the manuscript and suggested Fisher "tone it down."[38] The edits betray a lack of imagination. Beyond Fisher's put downs, a literary line like "At night, searchlights make sorcerous loveliness of the gardens" (to describe the gardens by the depot) would have been cut.

Fisher only lived in Boise during his employment with the FWP. For the rest of his life, he made his home in Hagerman, Idaho. He grew up in eastern Idaho, near Ririe, and had hoped to have his FWP offices in Pocatello, so he could be close to family. He

---

37. Bernard DeVoto, "The Writers' Project," *Harper's Magazine* 184 (January 1942), 220.

38. Boise Guide Editorial Report, Box A562, WPA Records, Library of Congress Manuscript Division. 220.

10097-M

EDITORIAL REPORT ON STATE COPY
(2 carbons required)

State Idaho   Date January 16, 1940

Subject Boise - Local Guide   Rating

    Considerable work is needed on this manuscript before it will be ready for publication. First of all there should be a careful pruning of material, inasmuch as the chronology is too long, and some of the points of interest are treated too lightly. It will be a case of taking away from one and building up the other so that a better balance may be struck. There is also throughout the text a type of flippant writing we suggest that you tone down. We have indicated numerous passages that we think should be deleted, and have no doubt that many more places can be found where condensation can be made.

    We think that our notations on the text will take care of most of the suggestions. However, in addition we offer the following:

    Under your Information for Tourists we suggest that you rearrange the material so that all items relating to transportation, recreation, etc., come together. Please be definite in giving information. Include addresses or locations for all points mentioned, and be specific.

    We suggest that the two items indicated under the statistical review be put under the information for tourists, and the rest of this section be dispensed with, since there is so much repetition here.

    The chronological treatment of the history is novel, and will be quite satisfactory when it is made more concise. There is too much petty information given here, along with the colorful stories. It should be thoroughly and carefully revised. Be careful not to include material that might be controversial.

    The points of interest section might be built up considerably, and we have indicated on the copy some changes in form.

    When the manuscript is revised please do not leave spaces for pictures. This can be taken care of when the book is finally made up.

Editorial report for The Boise Guide.

seems to care for Boise, but certainly doesn't love it as a hometown or a long-time resident would. Ultimately Fisher did like Boise; on the day of his resignation, the *Statesman* published an essay by Fisher in which he thanked the city for the time he spent here, and wished "for Boise all those things that give character and progressive growth to a city."[39]

The *Guide* is divided into four parts: Boise Today, Chronology, Points of Interest, and Tours in Environs. Fisher wrote the first part and the last two parts; the chronology was written by Milton Mills.

F. M. Tarr intended to make maps to be included in the *Guide*. (He was the same mapmaker for the other Idaho FWP books.) Those maps, if they were ever made, were not located. Fisher mentions that William Runyan did the drawings for the *Guide*; the only drawing located, however, was Runyan's draft for the cover of the guide. Extensive photographs, as Fisher desired, had apparently been selected for inclusion; he noted in the text where the photos should go. Those photographs also were not located. The photographs included in this volume are based on Fisher's wishes.

Alessandro Meregaglia is an assistant professor and archivist at Boise State University.

---

39. Vardis Fisher, "Vardis Fisher Is Taking to the Hills: Quitting Boise to Write Another Novel," *Idaho Statesman*, November 7, 1939, 1.

31

The Sonna Building at the corner of Ninth and Main in Boise, where Vardis Fisher had his office for the Federal Writers' Project on the second floor (79-45-2-12. Courtesy of the Idaho State Archives)

Editors' Note

The text of the *Guide* was transcribed directly from the manuscript at the Library of Congress. Few edits have been made to the text, except for clarity or minor grammatical changes. Fisher speaks frankly about race and does not hold back when describing the conditions in the city as he observed them.

It is not, and never will be, our intention to propagate the use of racial slurs or harmful stereotypes. However, we feel it is important to the integrity of this as a historical text to preserve the language and attitudes of the time in which it was written. Regardless of our distaste for some of the language used by Fisher, we have chosen not to disguise or ignore the injustices and prejudices revealed by his words that so many have experienced in this city in the past and continue to struggle against today.

The text has not been edited for factual accuracy. Fisher was not a historian. Indeed, though he wrote historical novels and historical essays, he tended not to use footnotes or carefully document his sources. This *Guide* is no exception. (Of his final book, *Gold Rushes and Mining Camps of the Early American West*, an editor of a journal criticized Fisher for his lack of careful documentation. He privately replied to a friend: "Pathetic how some persons get the notion that a large body of notes means scholarship."[40]) The *Guide* should be read for its commentary on and a snapshot of life in Boise in the 1930s during the Great Depression.

**Laura Wally Johnston &
Alessandro Meregaglia, 2019**

40. Fisher to David Stratton, January [15], 1968, Cage 4771, Vardis Fisher Letters, Manuscripts, Archives, and Special Collections, Washington State University Libraries.

34

The Boise Guide

By Vardis Fisher
and the Federal Writers' Project

Introduction

While it is intended that this guide to the capital city of Idaho will be of service chiefly to tourists and other visitors, it is hoped that it will bring to Boiseans a better knowledge of their city. To all Boiseans who helped to make this book, acknowledgement is given, and especially to President Eugene Chaffee of the Junior College, to Arthur H. Hays of Boise Senior High School, to Esther Hanifen of the State Historical Society, and to J. L. Driscoll of the First Security Bank.

Members of the Idaho Writers' Project staff to whom the book is particularly indebted include F. M. Tarr who drew the maps, William Runyan who contributed the drawings and Milton Mills who prepared the section on chronology.

Hotel Boise
(Courtesy of Mark Baltes)

Information for Tourists

Airport: Municipal airport is 6 m. Southwest of the city.

Accomodations:
Four large hotels in the business district and several smaller ones. Several de luxe auto camps just east or west of the city on U.S. 30. A great many restaurants, coffee

shops, and cafes, including a few which specialize in Basque, Chinese, or Scandinavian food.

Bus Stations: Union Pacific Stages, 215 N. 9th Street. Here also is the office of Scenic Stages, and Idaho Stage Company. The Mount Hood Stages' office is in the Grand Hotel, 11th and Main St. The Boise-Winnemucca Stages, Boise Hotel Stage Depot, 313 N. 8th St.

Boating: On the lagoon in Julia Davis Park.

Information Service:
The Boise Chamber of Commerce, 809 Idaho St.; the State Chamber of Commerce in the Idaho Building diagonally across from the Hotel Boise.

Cabarets: Idaho's system of State liquor control does not allow cabarets and night clubs to serve intoxicating drinks. In consequence, most of the places catering to night-life, such as the Country Club and certain hotels and restaurants, employ what is known as the locker-system. The patron rents a locker, buys his own liquor, and the establishment mixes and serves his drinks for him.

Golf: At the Boise Country Club southwest of the city; and at the Plantation 4 m. west of the city on State 44.

Highways: U.S. 30, the Old Oregon Trail highway, runs through Boise. Also leaving Boise on the west is State 44, and on the east is State 21. For other roads leading out (see Tours).

Hospitals: St. Luke's Hospital, 1st and Bannock; St. Alphonsus Hospital, 412 State.

Liquors: Only beer is available without a license, which costs 50¢ at the State Liquor Store, 112 S. 9th.

Ada Theater
(Courtesy of
Frank Aden Jr.)

Motion Picture House:

The principal one is the Ada at Main and 7th Streets. Others are the Pinney, Rialto, Granada, Lyric, and Rio.

Newspapers: The *Idaho Daily Statesman*, 603 Main Street; and the *Boise Capital News*, 713 Idaho Street.

Railroad Stations:

Union Pacific Station, at the

Pinney Theater (Courtesy of Mark Baltes)

southern end of Capitol Boulevard. City ticket office, 212 North Eighth.

Street Order: The principal street is Main which runs northwest-southwest, and on the southeast runs into and terminates in Warm Springs Avenue. North of it and running parallel are, in order: Idaho, Bannock, Jefferson, State; and parallel on the south are Grove and Front. Across the business district at right angles to Main are streets from First to Sixteenth numbered east to west.

Swimming: In the natatorium in White City Park at the eastern end of Warm Springs Avenue.

Boise Natatorium located on Warm Springs (Courtesy of Mark Baltes)

Traffic Regulations:
No U turns on Stop-streets, or on streets showing lights at intersection. Free parking on all streets, with time limit as indicated on posts or curb.

Taxis: Within the city proper the fare is 25¢ for one to four passengers.

Tennis: There are several excellent clay courts in Julia Davis Park.

Calendar of Annual Events

January: Idaho Wild-Life Conference
Charity Ball
President's Birthday Ball
Idaho Editorial Association Meeting
Idaho Woolgrowers' Convention

February: Chinese New Year
Lincoln Day Banquet
Shrine Ball

March: Basque Farewell Ball

April: Boise Junior College Prom

May: Music Week

June: National Guard Encampment

July:	Basque Picnic
August:	Idaho State Fair
September:	Idaho Medical Association Meeting
November:	Fireman's Ball Elk's Ball Idaho Education Association Meeting Opening of Community Concerts
December:	Policeman's Ball Sheepherder's Ball

Sheepherder's Ball, 1937 (Book 8, Juanita Uberuaga Hormaechea Scrapbooks. Courtesy of the Basque Museum & Cultural Center)

Pan-Hellenic Ball
Christmas Oratorio

Statistical Review

Form of government:
    Charter

Population: 1930: 21,544
    (Males: 10,522 / Females: 11,022.)

    1938: estimated 30,000

School census: 6,281

Area: five and one-fourth square miles

Altitude: 2,739 ft.

Parks: seven

Assessed valuation:
    $15,013,500.00 - Tax rate:
    $5.60 per hundred

Financial institutions:
    2 banks, 1 trust company,
    3 building and loan associations

Churches: 59, representing 22 denominations

Real estate: $6,747,000.00 - 70% of the homes owned by occupants

Principal industries:
agriculture, dairying, mining, lumbering

Trading area: retail, 50 miles radius with an estimated trading population of 60,000; wholesale, 150 miles radius with an estimated trading population of 200,000

Owyhee Hotel
(Courtesy of
Frank Aden Jr.)

Hotels:	eleven
Railroad:	one, the Union Pacific
Highways:	U.S. 30; State 44 and 21
Newspapers:	two, the *Idaho Daily Statesman* and the *Boise Capital News*
Radio stations:	two, KFXD and KIDO
Airports:	two, one at the intersection of Broadway and the river, and the other six miles south of the Union Pacific depot

KFXD radio station building in Nampa, Idaho (Courtesy of Art Gregory, History of Idaho Broadcasting Foundation)

Streets: total mileage, 118.4; paved, 67.5 miles

Telephones: 9,883

Water: Boise Water Co., private corporation. 7,025 users; 5,700,000 gallons daily capacity; 2,500,000 gallons used daily on an average; 112 miles of mains; value of plant, $2,546,990.00

Electricity: Idaho Power Co., unit of Electric Bond and Share Co. 11,207 power users

Fire department:
valuation, $26,388.70. Paid employees, 35; three ladder trucks in three station houses; chemical equipment and pump truck

Police department: valuation, $26, 388.70. Paid employees, 20; one station, seven pieces of motorized equipment

Ladies' Golf Day at Plantation Country Club (Courtesy of Plantation Country Club)

Union Pacific Stage Depot at Tenth and Main Street (79-45-3. Courtesy of the Idaho State Archives)

Idan-Ha Hotel (Courtesy of Mark Baltes)

Idaho State Capitol Building (Albert E. Nelson Photographs. Courtesy of Boise State Special Collections and Archives)

Hotel Boise (Courtesy of Mark Baltes)

Part I: Boise Today

Physical Aspect

As cities go, Boise is physically attractive, but it is the trees and not the buildings that make it so. Like cities everywhere, it suffers from want of congruity and planning structures, and so presents the appearance of having grown up in a burst of individualism, with no regard in any building for those around it. There is also, of course, the problem of changing tastes, from which all cities suffer so much in ugliness. The Idanha Hotel some thirty years ago was the edifice at which Boise pointed with greatest pride, but nobody finds it beautiful today. It has been supplanted in public esteem by the Hotel Boise; but perhaps in another thirty years this structure, which by common consent, would doubtless be placed next to the Capitol itself in pleasing architectural design, at least among the larger buildings, will be regarded as having the kind of old-fashioned stupidity that is today seen in the first automobiles.

Boise today is a monument to changing architectural styles that run the gamut from the pioneer cabin to all kinds of hybrids. Side by side are the hideous ornateness of the gingerbread era and the stripped simplicity of a mode that is a long way from gothic gargoyles. Upon any of several streets can be found enough incongruous architectural ineptness to abash any lover of the beautiful--if it were not for the trees, and it is the trees after all which give to Boise its somewhat legendary distinction of being one of the loveliest cities in the nation. Without them, the city would not inappropriately invite the metaphor of a peacock divested of it feathers.

Boise can take pride in its trees. With 85,000 of them, it has more than any other city in the country without an arboretum; and it owes a debt to Lafayette Cartee, a Frenchman with an arboricultural fever, who came to the spot in 1863 and decided that a town in so barren a desert ought to hide its drouth under foliage. The settlement he came to was a huddle of false-fronted shacks, hitching posts and dusty streets. Winds kalsomined everything with the topsoil from the arid sage-

Lafayette Cartee (74-50-3. Courtesy of the Idaho State Archives)

brush terrain westward. When Cartee was done, he had planted every kind of tree then grown in the Northwest, as well as species from the Orient, Europe and the eastern states. His enthusiasm lived in others who went on with the planting; and in consequence, Boise today has many long leafy avenues with ceilings arched over and dappled shadows upon the concrete.

Bird's eye view of Boise, 1890 (Courtesy of Boise State Special Collections and Archives)

When looked down upon from the northern hills, the city is seen as a solidly wooded residential district in the center of which is the business section, looking like a pile of children's blocks. The whole area is crowded into an elliptical bowl, and great mountains stretch to the very doorstep in a sheltering amphitheater which protects on all sides from violent wind and storm. Standing out is the Hotel Boise, impressive in its monolithic simplicity, and the Capitol, which has the customary lack of originality found in all buildings patterned after the parent in Washington, D. C. To the west is a valley of farms and orchards; and to the south is the barren tableland which water has not yet reclaimed.

The Streets

Part of Boise (the northwest section) is laid out on the compass; part of it (the business district) is upon the line of the river; and parts of the remainder show that the town, in growing, followed the trails and roads. The stranger, if he gets lost in so small a city, need not feel flabbergasted, for some of the residents have difficulty in finding their way around.

Capitol Boulevard, looking north, 1936 (Courtesy of Frank Aden Jr.)

The four principal streets are Main, which has always been the main street of the business district; Capitol Boulevard at the northern end of which stands the Capitol building and at the southern end, the

Main Street, looking east (Courtesy of Mark Baltes)

Main Street at night, looking west (Courtesy of Frank Aden Jr.)

Union Pacific station; Warm Springs Avenue, the eastern continuation of Main street, named for the hot springs found in its vicinity; and Harrison Boulevard in the northern part of the city. The last two are residential streets and along them are some of the most beautiful homes in the city.

Warm Springs Avenue (Courtesy of Mark Baltes)

Looking west from the top of the Owyhee Hotel (Courtesy of Mark Baltes)

Eighth and Main Streets at night (Courtesy of Mark Baltes)

Grove street, the first one south of Main, was named for the trees which lined it; for in its heyday this street was the swankiest in the town. Today it is bordered chiefly by old ramshackle buildings. In the extreme southeastern part of the city are streets named for trees, such as Elm, Maple, Walnut and Locust; in the northwestern end are streets named for women, including Dora, Irene, Bella, Hazel and Ada. The male of the species are only represented by Wilbur and Bruce. Other streets are named for families who were

Aerial view of the State Capitol and Hotel Boise, looking northeast (Courtesy of Mark Baltes)

prominent in the early history of the town. Among them are Lemp, Ridenburg, Eastman, O'Farrell, Hays, Brumback, Anderson, Miller, Gavin, Lee, Stewart, Ellis, Regan, Lewis, Borah, Good, Costin, Sherman and Haines. Other street names include River, Grand, Park, Fairview, Flume, Pioneer, Pleasanton, Woodlawn and Sunset.

Eighth and Idaho Streets at night (Courtesy of Mark Baltes)

Natural Setting

Boise is situated in southwestern Idaho about 35 miles east of the Idaho-Oregon line, and about 95 miles north of Nevada. It stands at an elevation of 2,739 feet at the eastern end of Boise Valley. The

Boise river and Table Rock (Courtesy of Mark Baltes)

Boise river, constantly shifting its course, has formed numerous islands, the largest of which is Eagle island downstream from the city. While there are numerous creeks feeding the river in its upper stretch, the only important tributary within the valley is Indian Creek. Small tributaries running through the city are Cottonwood Creek and Sand Creek; and occasionally, when augmented by heavy rains or rapidly melting snow, these overwhelm their banks and flood streets and basements. Since the construction of Arrowrock Reservoir, the river rarely floods.

Black lava, embossed with green lichen, covers the slopes up the canyon east of the city, and indicates intermittent flows during the volcanic periods. In early days, veins of quartz found here were rich in gold, and some gold is still found in the river bed. A small plateau of lava east of the city, known as Table Rock (see Tour 1), is an old landmark. East and north of Table Rock are the high, and in their lower reaches denuded, mountains of the Boise Ridge. Shafer Butte rises to an elevation of 7,591 feet.

Rotary Club outing at Shafer Butte lookout, 1920 (61-122-37. Courtesy of the Idaho State Archives)

The river bottom soil near the city is sandy with washed quartz cobblestones in abundance just under the surface. This type of soil lends itself to truck gardening; and even formerly, when only Indians roamed the valley, supported a luxuriant growth of indigenous poplar and cottonwood and willow. Geologists declare that the whole basin may once have been a great lake, a remnant of an inland sea that covered a large area in which Great Salt Lake today is the most notable survivor. Legends suggest that Indians used to paddle canoes 40 feet or more above the present valley floor. The benchland or mesa south and southwest of the city is underlain by the same lakebed sand, but the surface is heavy gumbo soil. Low barren foothills are in the north.

Before magic irrigation, Boise Valley was a semi-arid desert. The coyote and jackrabbit have vanished with the sagebrush in the farmed areas; but the gopher, to the dismay of farmers, remains and burrows tunnels that often play havoc with ditches and canals. Nut trees in the city have attracted many friendly squirrels; and in the foliage along the streets are chiefly robins, Rocky Mountain bluebirds and western canaries. In the open, commonest birds are the meadowlark, kildeer, and the ubiquitous English sparrow. Teal and mallard ducks are natural. Trout swim in the river side by side with sucker and carp. The mormon cricket (Anabrus simplex) does not seem to have prospered until farmers

View of the Foothills northwest (Courtesy of Mark Baltes)

began to raise things that it found more to its taste; and today, after mild winters, hordes of the insect introduce themselves to the valley in locust plagues.

In the hills and desert roundabout are many varieties of wild flowers. Along ditch banks are sourdock, sweet clover, burdock, Spanish needles and sometimes the poisonous hemlock. Common in the desert are the ragweed, tumbleweed, and the Russian thistles, the last of which, an almost ineradicable pest, came with agriculture.

Boise has an exceptional record of freedom from earthquake, tornado and hurricane. Slight seismic disturbances have been recorded but none of them

243. View looking Northeast from the Dome of the Capitol, Boise, Idaho.

View of the Foothills northeast (Courtesy of Mark Baltes)

has been severe enough to destroy property. The highest wind velocity measured by the weather bureau was 43 miles per hour in June of 1900. Boise temperatures are generally very mild. The highest on record was 121 degrees in 1871; the lowest was 28 degrees below zero in 1888. The average mean temperature for the past 72 years is 51.3 degrees. The annual humidity average ranges from 70% at six o'clock in the morning to 43% at six o'clock in the evening. The average annual

Capitol Boulevard, looking south (Courtesy of Mark Baltes)

precipitation during the 72 years recorded has been 13.08 inches. The average annual hours of sunshine have been 3,028. The growing season usually begins in April and runs for an average of 170 days.

Racial Elements[1]

See Editors' note, pg 32.

Perhaps the first racial type to inhabit what is now Boise was Indian. Early travelers reported wigwam villages along the Boise River, and historians assume that Indians encamped where the city is now. Today, however, a Redskin in Boise is about as rare as zero weather.

The first group of early settlers was chiefly of war-weary southerners. Other yankees came; but the racial components were indistinguishable until the advent of the Chinese. They came in hordes to work exhausted mining claims and were so prosperous that the Territorial Legislature of 1864 taxed them four dollars a month for the privilege of making money from spots that the whites had exploited and left as worthless. Besides taxing them to death, old-timers also accused them of countless crimes which they never committed; and thought no more of blowing their brains out than of hanging white thugs to a bridge beam or a tree. But in spite of all persecutions, the Chinese increased in number and prospered, and by 1890 compromised a considerable part of the town's business district. Some, preferring a quieter life, rented fertile garden plots in the Davis tract westward and grew succulent vegetables. On Idaho Street, back of the city hall, was a three-story building which housed the Masonic temple; and down the street were cellars and sub-cellars and tunnels which were used in the opium trade. Opium was legal then; and as late as 1897, photographs showed Chinese lying around on tables and inhaling through long bamboo pipes.

Boise still has its Chinese population, some of whom are still noted for the quality of vegetables they produce. The green checkerboard of gardens on the Davis tract, tilled formerly by old gnarled fingers that crushed the soil, now trembles under the roar of gasoline tractors; and the decrepit shacks that once housed withered

Hip Sing Association Building (75-104-1. Courtesy of the Idaho State Archives)

old men are now used for storage. The gaunt old horses that pulled the umbrella-covered wagons have been replaced by modern trucks that race from door to door to make deliveries. Nothing remains of the old ways except the pidgin English; and this the Chinese cannily keep because of its commercial value. They sell more if they can say, "Solly, no gottee cellots but gottee colleflow tloday."

Chinese New Year Parade, 1911 (76-18-9. Courtesy of the Idaho State Archives)

The largest foreign group with preservation of native customs and language is the Basques. The colony here is said to be the largest in the western world. These people are a proud race who kept their ancient tribal signs, customs, and a language that may date back to the Age of Bronze. When Caesar conquered Gaul, he found the Basques too much for him; nor has any tyrant since been able to crush this group stemming from the ancestral estates high in the Pyrenees. Possibly the first Basque settlers in North America came to the Jordan Valley in Oregon and moved from there into Idaho to engage in their raising of sheep.

American Basque Fraternity Auxiliary, 1933 (Book 29, Juanita Uberuaga Hormaechea Scrapbooks. Courtesy of the Basque Museum & Cultural Center)

Today the younger Basques care little about preserving their language and customs. Names like Yriondo, Gabica, and Domingo remain; but there is more and more intermarriage, and less disposition to exclude strangers from their annual celebrations. The gingham-and-overall Sheepherders' Ball at Christmas time is now open to anyone who wishes to attend; and such old Basque folk dances as La Jota as likely as not alternate with modern dances. There are Basque restaurants but they now serve other food as well.

Other foreign or racial groups in Boise are very small. The few Negroes are not segregated, though they are excluded from some of the dance halls and restaurants. There are a few Croatians and Austrians who came during the construction of Arrowrock Dam,

Traditional Basque dancing (2015.054.022. Courtesy of the Basque Museum & Cultural Center)

but to a large extent their national identity has been lost in the melting pot.

The Press

The oldest newspaper in Boise is the *Idaho Daily Statesman*, founded on the 15th of July, 1864, only a year after the town had been laid out. Establishment of the newspaper was largely fortuitous; because it was only by chance that three men, riding in a wagon carrying a printing press, stopped in the new village to inquire the way. They drew up in front of the Riggs and Agnew livery stable and announced that they were going to Idaho City. Idaho City, though a ghost now, was a booming city of fifteen thousand then, whereas Boise was a fresh little mining camp of three hundred. In Boise, nevertheless, were some merchants who could smell an opportunity when it was right under their noses; and they persuaded the men to set up their shop in their town.

The *Statesman*'s first issue appeared on July 26, a four-column tri-weekly that saluted the village with this announcement: "We shall in the first place try to make the *STATESMAN* a news paper that everybody in the Territory can afford to buy and if possible, one that few can afford to do without."

The price was a dollar a week, twenty dollars a year. Those were the days when news of the Civil War, even though two weeks or a month old, was eagerly read.

Idaho Statesman building, ca. 1933 (60-1-22. Courtesy of the Idaho State Archives)

Those were the days, too, when it was customary to throw roses at rival newspapers with the first announcement, and heave bricks from then on. *The Statesman* declared itself to be staunchly Republican, against all rebels, and resolved to have at anything or anyone associated with 'Rebeldom.' Many secessionists who had come here to escape from the brutalities of war found the caustic editorials not at all to their taste; and in November of 1867 a newspaper was founded to represent the interests of the Democratic party.

It was called the *Boise Democrat*, and as soon as the polite formalities of the salutation were over, the war began in earnest. The editors called one another liars so often that the word almost became meaningless. Waxing hot under the collar, the *Statesman* said: "We shall not be accused of the pretense of seeking to contradict what every lying cur has to say about us or the *STATESMAN*." Persons read both papers not only for news of war or the chronicles of local gossip or the homely proverbs of Josh Billings, but also to learn what fresh epithet or what noisome insinuation was being hurled at a rival editor. Secessionist feeling became so strong in the town that the owner of the *Statesman* deemed it wise to sell out to his competitor; whereupon matters ran smoothly for a while except for the aftermath of scorn for all Republicans. The Republicans were not asleep. They struck back by refusing to take advertising space, and the *Statesman* went back to its original owner. His editorials thereupon suggested that a rest had revitalized him, for he lambasted his foes with the energy of Popeye the Sailor.

From that time on other newspapers appeared

and vanished. Among them were the *Boise Democrat*, already mentioned, as well as *The Capital*, *The Chronicle*, *The Idahoan*, *The Republican*, and the *Idaho Democrat*. Later issues invigorated editors, but none more than the fight for free silver: it was this lively brawl that led to the *Silver Champion*, which was followed by *The Capital* in the initial issue in which appeared this announcement: "*The Capital* is the earnest champion of silver and the uncompromising foe of the single gold standard."

Judge Kelly, an ardent Republican, had purchased the *Statesman* in 1872, and in 1888 it became the first daily. *The Capital* was a daily too, and the war was on again. The first, indeed, between the *Statesman* and the early *Democrat* was only child's tomfoolery in comparison with the feud which now developed. The *Statesman* liked to talk of the 'dam fool' policies of the Democrats, then in power in the state, and never missed a chance to score the 'harebrained' Bryan, and the 'hazy, impossible' issues of populism and free silver. *The Capital* called the *Statesman* a 'goldbug' sheet, said its editors were liars, and rarely printed an issue without a quotation from Bryan.

In 1901, the *Capital* became the *Idaho Capital News*. Later, it was the *Evening Capital News*, but today it is the *Boise Capital News*. The *Idaho Capital News* was edited by R. S. Sheridan of whom it was said by both friends and enemies that he was a fighting fool. After he was injured and lost his old fire, the pioneer Dewey family took control by virtue of a sheriff's sale. The new management saw eye to eye with the *Statesman* in so many things that the city lost interest, and the *Idaho Capital News* found itself headed for bankruptcy. It was then bought by the Scripps League of Newspapers.

Calvin Cobb, at right, with his wife and children (60-1-4. Courtesy of the Idaho State Archives)

In recent years, the *Statesman* has been managed and owned by Calvin Cobb, one of Boise's most memorable and implacable characters. Regarded by some as a hopeless reactionary, he nevertheless was the first newspaper editor in Idaho to sign agreements with organized labor and to give a living wage to his staff. He declared he was sorry he supported suffrage for women and the direct primary; and added that he was opposed to free silver for six months and 'had a hell of a time.' Today, the *Statesman* is owned and managed by his daughter [Margaret Cobb Ailshie], who, some have opined, is a chip off the old block. Its editor is Irving W. Hart, a handsome giant who likes to make the ink hot when he settles down to the caustic job of lampooning anyone or anything which he thinks needs a good drubbing. *The Boise Capital News* is edited by Saxton Bradford, also handsome, who can raise more steam than his soft-spoken manner would suggest, and is managed by Taylor Robertson who has been on the staff for twenty years.

Margaret Cobb Ailshie (75-81-1A. Courtesy of the Idaho State Archives)

But Boise is no longer the old west, and its newspaper editors no longer call one another liars. If the two newspapers carry on any of the feud that used to make readers pull their hair and renew their subscription, it is too subtly hidden to be recognized. The *Statesman* is still Republican, the *News* is independent with a leaning to the Democrats; but the old give-and-take with no holds barred battles of the predecessors are as dead as the Chinese joss house.

Taylor Robertson, 1939 (62-20-18767, R. Harold Sigler Collection. Courtesy of the Idaho State Archives)

Radio

It was in 1922 that Harry Redeker, an instructor of chemistry in the Boise high school, determined to build a radio broadcasting station. He assembled pieces of junk and converted them into an apparatus that became the pride of the community; because Redeker's amateur hour broadcasting was picked up as far away as Hawaii, Alaska, and steamships in the Pacific Ocean. In 1928 the equipment was sold, and a more pretentious station, called KIDO, was set up in the Elk's Building. Though it featured local talent only, it is said to have been the first commercial station between the Mississippi River and the Pacific Coast.

Boise High School, 1934 (Courtesy of Boise High School)

It was moved later into the basement of the Hotel Boise, and in 1937 to the mezzanine floor. In the same year it was hooked up with the NBC network. Today with 2,500 watts, it is the most powerful privately owned station in the country. It broadcasts on a frequency of 1,350 kilocycles. On the mezzanine floor of the Owyhee Hotel is a remote-control branch of station KFXD of Nampa, which broadcasts 250 watts of power

KIDO Advertisement (Courtesy of Art Gregory, History of Idaho Broadcasting Foundation)

on 1,200 kilocycles. Its specialty is transcription programs.

In addition to these two commercial stations there are approximately seventy licensed amateur radio operators in the city.

Industries

Boise is not an industrial city but chiefly a wholesale distributing center for goods manufactured elsewhere. Its natural mineralized hot water,

Interior of the Boise Natatorium (Courtesy of Mark Baltes)

with a daily flow of 1,200,000 gallons, has been developed in a natatorium at the end of Warm Springs Avenue, but more importantly to heat a great many Boise homes. It contains twelve minerals, and has a natural temperature of 170 degrees F. Just East of the city are the sandstone quarries (see Tour 1) which formerly were active but now are seldom exploited.

Barber Dam and Lumber Mill (Courtesy of Mark Baltes)

Among the small industries with the city, the principal ones are companies producing lumber, ice, candy, ice cream, bakery goods, various building materials, nonalcoholic beverages, iron and other metal products, and tents and awnings. Until recently, the

West-Rest Company, manufacturing Oregon Trail furniture, was established here, and became nationally famous for the unusual quality of its products.

Crane moving sandstone at Table Rock Quarry (73-2-31D. Courtesy of the Idaho State Archives)

Tramway at Table Rock Quarry, ca. 1914 (76-114-2a. Courtesy of the Idaho State Archives)

Churches

Christ Chapel at Fifteenth and Ridenbaugh Streets, 1963 (AR 000573. Courtesy of Boise State Special Collections and Archives)

Boise has an extraordinary number of churches for a city of its size. Legend declares that the first services were held in 1863 in the historic O'Farrell cabin which now stands on Fort street. In August of that year, the Rev. Michael Fackler came to the village and began Episcopal services in the schoolhouse. He was largely instrumental in the building of the first church [Christ Chapel], dedicated in 1866 at the corner of what is now Seventh and Bannock streets, but standing today at Fifteenth and Ridenbaugh. An inscription on its bronze tablet declares that it was the first Protestant church in Montana, Idaho, and Utah. By 1865, Methodists, Catholics, and Baptists were all holding regular services in the town.

The first Catholic house of worship stood between Third and Fourth Streets on Jefferson where St. Teresa's Academy now stands. After it burned down, the cathedral at Eighth and Fort was erected in 1906, a large and impressive structure in French Gothic. Catholics have recently completed St. Mary's Church at Twenty-Sixth and State Streets, and though it looks a little like a barn with a high loft, it is said to be truly representative of old English Gothic.

The first church building in Boise served the Episcopalians until 1902 when the church was rectory at Eighth and state streets were completed. The Bishop Tuttle house, serving as church school and a recreational hall, was built in 1907. Next to these is a Deanery; and three English Gothic structures of Idaho stone, now green with ivy, make a quaintly beautiful block.

Baptist Church at Tenth and Jefferson Streets (Courtesy of Mark Baltes)

Baptist services began in the old court house which used to stand on the site of the present City Hall. In 1866 a church was erected a Ninth and Idaho Streets at a cost of $2,500, but the pastor became more interested in

Architectural rendering of the Cathedral of St. John the Evangelist (Courtesy of Mark Baltes)

beekeeping than in preaching and the Methodists thereupon possessed the building. The present Baptist church at Tenth and Jefferson was dedicated in 1892. Meanwhile, a Methodist preacher came in 1872 to find his flock "without church-house, Sunday school or organ." Meetings were held in the Good Templar Hall at Sixth and Main Streets until a church was built at Eighth and Bannock Streets in 1874. The present church at the corner of Tenth and State Streets is a brick structure that cost $50,000.

Methodist Church at Tenth and State Streets (Courtesy of Mark Baltes)

It was in the early Methodist building that the Presbyterian church was organized in 1878. Later, meetings were held in the Baptist church until a house was erected at Tenth and Main Streets where the Idan-Ha Hotel now stands. The building at Ninth and State Streets was completed in 1893, and since then an annex has been added. Congregationalists also held their first meetings in the Baptist structure. In 1891 they met in the G. A. R. hall on State between Seventh and Eighth Streets; but five years later a chapel was built, and it still serves as part of the present church.

Second Ward LDS Chapel, located on Main Street between 3rd and 4th Streets, 1939 (PH 211. Courtesy of the Church History Library, Church of Jesus Christ of Latter-Saints)

No picture of churches in southern Idaho would be complete without a word about the Mormons. It is said that the first Mormons in Boise came as prisoners to the penitentiary during those years when every Mormon was suspected of having a score of wives and was thrown into jail if he could be captured. Mormon missionaries came to Boise in 1897 and bought from the Campbellites a frame structure at Fourth and Jefferson which is still in use. In 192[4] a tabernacle as erected at Ninth and Washington at a cost of $85,000. At this writing, the Mormons are putting up two modern structures in the city one at Fourth and Main and the other on the Whitney Bench.

Congregation Ahavath Beth Israel (HABS ID,1-BOI-SE,11--1. Courtesy of the Library of Congress)

Among the fifty-nine churches in Boise representing twenty-two denominations are the Jewish synagogue at Eleventh and State, and the Bethel African Methodist Episcopal building at Eighteenth and Idaho, the latter of which is distinguished by an excellent choir. From 1902 until 1937 there was a Chinese temple at the corner of Seventh and Front Streets, the gilded and flowery interior of which was open to Buddhist, Shintoist or Taoist.

Architectural rendering of the Boise Stake LDS Tabernacle, 1924 (PH 211. Courtesy of the Church History Library, Church of Jesus Christ of Latter-Saints)

Schools

The Territorial Legislature of 1863 started off with a platitude as worn as a Roman highway: "Let us establish schools, encourage teachers, patronize the arts and sciences, teach our children to seek knowledge rather than wealth." Even so, that was a bold statement in a frontier area of gamblers and salon-keepers, miners bent on getting drunk, and cattlemen and sheepmen most of whom were soured old bachelors. Very few persons saw any need of schooling the young, and in consequence most of the early schools were privately owned. In 1864 it was announced in the *Statesman* by one of these enterprising pedagogues that he could teach anyone penmanship so flawless that correspondents would not go crazy trying to decipher epistles from Boise. By 1865 the *Statesman*'s editor was campaigning for a public school system, but persons gave no heed except to study his diction and rhetoric.

The Territorial Legislature did nothing. They kicked the public school bills around until they wore them out or lost them. A tax of one percent to support schools was collected by the sheriff and he retained six-tenths of it as his commission. Even at that, he did not become wealthy. The legislature in

1881 created the Boise Independent School District. Thereupon a board was elected, and an ornate building set up to the disgust and dismay of a considerable number of tax-payers. A graduate of Bates College in Maine was invited to become superintendent, which he did so with such lusty regard for sound applications of the hickory stick that he was forced to resign. It was foolishness, in the first place, to want to educate the sons and the daughters of parents who had done very well without education; and it was downright folly to try to flog them into learning. Nevertheless the American craze for education, by this time a world phenomenon, had its way and the tax-payers had to yield.

Whittier school was completed in 1894, a homely red brick unit of four rooms. In 1898 a second story was added, and today the building stands at Twelfth and Fort Streets, one of the historic landmarks of the city. In 1917 the roof was burned off and since then the building has suffered neglect. A survey of Boise schools in 1920 declared the building to be unsanitary and the grounds insufficient, but it held its own until 1936 when it was taken over by a division of the Works Progress Administration. Today, serious adults ponder the inscrutable problems of the world where thirty years ago unruly youngsters spent most of their time plotting new ways to flabbergast their teachers.

Two years after the Whittier was built the district was again overcrowded; and as a consequence the Lincoln school was built at Fourth and Idaho. It has a facade of mixed parentage, topped by pineapple spires. A Caldwell contractor by name of Miller agreed to erect it for $15,000 but went broke and fled, leaving his bondsmen to finish the job. Today, Lincoln is the district's 'opportunity' school for pupils who need special instruction.

Lincoln Elementary School (Courtesy of Mark Baltes)

The northwest part of town began to howl and in 1897 the Washington was built at Fifteenth and Ridenbaugh. It was a two-story frame building that went up in flames in 1917 and was replaced by a red brick structure. Now the southwest part of town clamored and a school, the Park School, was erected to which an addition was made in 1911. By this time the district called South Boise was up in arms. Toward the close of the century an eight-room building costing $20,000 had almost bankrupted the taxpayers there; but since then they prospered and now have a plain, well-constructed unit called the Garfield. The architecture is so simple that, from the outside, this building looks like nothing so much as a huge cube of brick.

Directly east of Boise was another district. For a while it had a two-story structure that enjoyed

Park Elementary School (Courtesy of Mark Baltes)

Garfield Elementary School, 1900 (69-4-28. Courtesy of the Idaho State Archives)

the distinction of being heated by natural hot water; but today that edifice, called the Hawthorne, is used as a storage vault. More recent structures over the city include the New Central at Seventh and Washington, the Longfellow at Ninth and Ada, the Roosevelt at Jefferson and Elm, the Lowell at Twenty-eight and Heron, and the Whitney on a bench south and the Collister on a bench west of the town.

The foregoing are all grade schools. High school was begun in the old central building, and when it was overflowed, a part of the present structure was built on Washington between Tenth and Eleventh. In an attempt to get a fancy design from the East, the board

Boise High School Auditorium, 1932 (Courtesy of Boise High School)

scorned local architects and got a building for their pains that almost precipitated a war. Haste was made in 1910 to add the east wing, and the west wing followed in 1912; so that today, at a cost of $434,000.00 the entire edifice looks a little better than it did when only the center part stood as a monument to the notions of a gentlemen east of the Mississippi. The auditorium, largest in the city, seats 1,472. In 1920 an industrial arts building was erected across the street; and in 1937 an excellent gymnasium was completed. In this year, too, was completed the **Junior High School** at Twelfth and Fort Streets, perhaps the finest school building in the city.

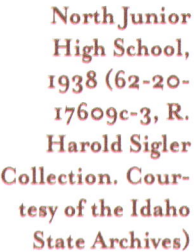

North Junior High School, 1938 (62-20-17609c-3, R. Harold Sigler Collection. Courtesy of the Idaho State Archives)

First Day of Boise Junior College, 1932 (AR 009742. Courtesy of Boise State Special Collections and Archives)

The first parochial school was held in 1867 in the Episcopal church. It grew so rapidly that it outdistanced the public schools and in 1871 had sixty pupils. In 1890 St. Margaret's, a school for girls, was established upon the site of the present Boise Junior College. In 1831 the buildings were offered to Boise for a college, but too many canny persons, already taxed to death, declined to accept. Undaunted, the Rev. Middleton Barnwell himself opened a junior college in 1932, officially sponsored by the Episcopal Church. By 1934 the taxpayers re-

Middleton Barnwell, First President of Boise Junior College (AR 029254. Courtesy of Boise State Special Collections and Archives)

lented and assumed the responsibility, and today some of them are entertaining the notion that a city of 25,000 persons ought to be able to support a four-year college.

St. Margaret's School (Courtesy of Mark Baltes)

St. Teresa's Academy architectural rendering by J. E. Tourtellotte & Co. (Charles Frederick Hummel Papers. Courtesy of Boise State Special Collections and Archives)

The only other parochial school of importance is St. Teresa's Academy at 312 Jefferson St. It was founded in 1889 by five Holy Cross Sisters from Notre Dame, and since then has grown rapidly. In 1934 its doors were also opened to boys of high school age.

The Arts

Boise's greatest achievement in the arts is perhaps Music Week, which since its beginning in 1919 has become almost a national institution. Cities in increasing numbers are adopting the festival as their own. Boise's Music Week, a community enterprise, is held annually in May. The first week took its form from the Boise Choral Society and allied groups. An offspring of the Society, the Boise Civic Festival Chorus, now operates with other musical organizations

Boise Music Week performance, 1933 (Courtesy of Boise Music Week and Justin Webb)

in building Boise's various musical interests into a grand finale in which the emphasis is more on the inspiration and joy of the participants than on the audience.

Allied groups include the Municipal Band, the men's Glee Club, the Madrigal Club, the Tuesday Musical Club, and the Singing Mothers. The Boise Civic Festival Chorus gives an oratorio annually during the Christmas holidays. Assistance comes too from all the churches which are devoted to music and have their own choirs. Indeed, music in Boise is promoted with extraordinary energy and earnestness; and musicians who come in from outside the state always face capacity houses.

The Boise Art Association, with small branches throughout the State, holds memberships in the American Federation of Arts and in the Western Association of Art; and since its organization in 1931 has promoted several nationally known art exhibits. The gallery was first in the First National Bank Building, then in the Carnegie Library, but is now in a handsome structure of its own in Julia Davis Park. The Association presents annual hangings of work by Idaho artists. Among the painters in Boise are Cornelia Hart and Ethel Lucille Fowler, both of whom placed canvasses in the second All-American Artist Show in New York City. Reeves Euler has had landscapes hung in the Biennial exhibition in Washington, D. C. and in the exhibition of the Princeton Art Association. Mary Hollingshed has had hangings in Seattle, Los Angeles and Cleveland. Estella Evans has exhibited landscapes in galleries in Chicago. Keith Hart specializes in marionettes for dramatization. A Boise Sketching Club has about forty members.

Boise Art Museum, 1940 (Ms511-319-1a, Everett L. "Shorty" Fuller Photograph Collection. Courtesy of the Idaho State Archives)

In sculpture Boise has not done so well. Robert Dunlap has made busts of Will Rogers and others and shows unmistakable promise. The most unique piece that has been done is the equestrian statue of George Washington which stands in the rotunda of the Capitol. Charles Ostner, a Hungarian who came to Idaho in 1862, carved it out of yellow pine, using as tools a common axe, saw, chisel and gouge. He labored on it during many an evening between 1864 and 1868 while his son held a pitch pine torch and Ostner used a postage stamp for a model. The finished carving was smoothed with glass and sandpaper, gilded with Bronze paint, and overlaid with gold leaf. For Sixteen years it stood in wind and storm at the intersection of Seventh and Idaho Streets; and then for fifty-one years stood on the east side of the capitol grounds, still unprotected, before in 1936 it was moved inside.

Charles Ostner's statue inside the Capitol (64-36-1. Courtesy of the Idaho State Archives)

Boise has been represented by only a few writers of any prominence. Glenn Balch writes books for boys and contributes to various magazines. Mrs. Jack Skillern [Helen Regan Skillern] is the author of *Flames from a Candle*; Frances Sweet Leonard of *When Evening Shadows Fall*; Wallace David Gillis of [The Idaho Legislature]. Jane Redfield Hoover, Donna Wayland, Mrs. Earl Turner [Faith Bailey Turner] have contributed widely to magazines; and others, including Eugene Chafee, Norman B. Adkison, Della Adams Leitner, Ida M. Gillett Durnim, Claire Boyle Bracken, Cedric [Dick] d'Easum, and Mrs. George Buhn [Mina Clark Buhn] are feature writers of more than local note. Della Adams Leitner has also had poems in several anthologies.

Glenn Balch and Vardis Fisher, 1968 (Vardis and Opal Fisher Papers. Courtesy of Boise State Special Collections and Archives)

In drama Boise had a little theater which, at this writing, is still struggling to survive. Besides it, plays are annually presented by the Boise High School Dramatic Club and by the LDS dramatic organizations. The WPA dramatic society has for its coach Della Pringle who appeared on the stage for fifty years and formerly organized and directed play companies of her own.

Della Pringle, seated third from right, with her all-female WPA drama group in Boise, 1938 (Courtesy of The Theatre Museum of Repertoire Americana, Mount Pleasant, Iowa)

Parks and Playgrounds

Original entrance to Julia Davis Park (Courtesy of Mark Baltes)

It took Boiseans a long time to recognize the advantages of a park system; but today, after the awakening, Boise has in Julia Davis Park a most ambitious project for a city so small. There are thirteen other parks, but they are no more than attractive pastures with a few trees. Thomas Davis gave a considerable part of the present Julia Davis area to the city in 1907 when he observed that the only outdoor recreation spot, Riverside Park, was falling into the river. Thereupon persons patriotically and energetically dumped tin cans and other trash on the low areas in the new park so that it would not sink out of sight like its predecessor. They dumped so much trash that they forgot all about Elm Grove Park at Twenty-Second and Irene Streets and left it to the tyranny of weeds; allowed the fashionably country club, Pierce Park, west of the city, to return to its primitive condition; planted alfalfa in Memorial Park at Fifth and Hays Streets so that farmers could harvest it; and in the Municipal Tourist Park at the South end of Walnut Street, they planted cottonwood and poplar trees so

Riverside Park
(Courtesy of Mark Baltes)

Municipal Tourist Park
(Courtesy of Mark Baltes)

that the grass, in being shaded, would never grow tall enough to have to be mowed. The cemeteries, meanwhile, were well taken care of. And even now, the Children's Park at Fifth and Grove is a wretched waste of yellow; sand and weeds, but the grass is lush and carefully trimmed around the graves of the dead.

Except in Julia Davis Park, Boise offers little in the way of outdoor recreation. There is a large natatorium at the end of Warm Springs Avenue where persons can frolic in natural hot water. The Basques have two handball courts. There are golf courses beyond the city limits. For the most part, Boiseans go out of the city to seek their playgrounds, chiefly to McCall, Pine View, Arrowrock Dam and other points to the north.

Municipal Tourist Park campgrounds (Courtesy of Mark Baltes)

Barber dam
aerial view
(Courtesy of
Mark Baltes)

Part II: Chronology

Prepared with Milton Mills

Prehistory

The more obvious features of Boise's topography were laid down in the period when boiling lava was deposited, layer after layer, to a depth of four hundred feet. Some thousands of years later, the waters of the receding glacial age completely covered the valley. After the waters drained away into the Pacific, a long period of quiescence set in, which left the valley in its present condition. The sediment left by the water, together with the slowly disintegrating lava ash, made a marvelously fertile soil. On account of the lack of rainfall, however, prairie grass and sagebrush were the only flora hardy enough to thrive. The surrounding mountains, receiving more rain, developed flora similar to that found in the more moist Pacific coast zone.

Little is known as to when the first aborigines occupied this territory. No discoveries of archaeological significance have been made. Indian petroglyphs and fragments of pottery are abundant, but do not date back more than four hundred years, according to expert opinion. The prominent landmark, now known as Table Rock, which rises at the eastern end of' the city, was used as an Indian lookout, and for at least several centuries before the white man came, Indian smoke signals rose from its summit. In the valley below, the river meadows undoubtedly were a favorite camping ground for the nomadic tribes of the Shoshoni Indians.

1805

The first knowledge of Boise valley was gained by the explorers Lewis and Clark, who did not see it, but received a second-hand account of it from the Indians. The Lewis and Clark map indicates the course of Boise river with fair accuracy, and labels it the Coppoppabash, said to mean "place of the cottonwoods."

1811

On November 21, Wilson Price Hunt, 30-year old commercial adventurer, became the first white man to actually visit the Boise River. Hunt led the transcontinental march of the Astorian party, financed by America's first millionaire, John Jacob Astor.

1812

As far as is known, Hunt did not assign any name to the Boise River on his westward trip; but eight months later a group of the same Astorians retraced the way, going eastward to carry dispatches to J. J. Astor, and according to the journal of Robert Stewart the river was then designated as "Wooded River," or as Rivere Boisee by the French-Canadian in the party. This is the origin of the name Boise, although a local legend erroneously ascribes it to Captain Bonneville (who did not arrive on Boise River until 20 years later).

1813

The first attempt to establish white men's habitations in Boise Valley ended in a mysterious orgy of bloodshed. One section of the Astorians, under the brave veteran John Reed, came into the Boise valley in the fall of 1813 for a winter of beaver trapping. But about the first of January 1814, Reed and his twelve men were mercilessly butchered, supposedly by a band of Indians whose identity had never become known. The only survivor was the Dorion Woman, who happened to be some distance away preparing supper for the men at the time of the attack. For many years after this event, the Rivere Boisee was often called Reed's River; early maps frequently spell it "Reid."

1819

Complications that arose out of the war of 1812 forced Astor to abandon his grandiose projects in the Oregon country. A Canadian organization, the Northwest Company, rushed in to monopolize the fur trade. Strangely enough, the first trader who entered Boise valley under the British-Canadian dispensation was an ex-Astorian, Donald McKenzie.

1821

In this year the Northwest Company was absorbed by the older Hudson's Bay Company, and many trappers lost their employment. McKenzie, however, received a handsome advancement, which took him back to Canada. His successors, most of whom made annual trapping ventures through Boise Valley, were Finan McDonald, 1823; Alexander Ross, 1824; Peter Skene Ogden, 1825-30; John Work 1830-31; and Francis Ermatinger, 1832-35.

1824
The Hudson's Bay Company enjoyed but briefly the uncontested spoils of the inland fur empire; in 1824 American trappers began re-invading the Far West. The first and most picturesque of these American mountain men was the astoundingly young Jedediah Strong Smith, whose passion for the Bible was second only to his passion for adventure.

1829
By 1829 there were said to be as many as six hundred Americans trapping in Idaho. Their ruthless annihilation of the beaver soon brought the golden age of the fur trade to an ignominious end.

1833
Captain B.L.E. Bonneville, on furlough from the U.S Army, brought his band of fur traders to the headwaters of the Boise River. It is doubtful whether he was ever on the site of the present city, as he found the desirable region already occupied by a group of American trappers. This was his usual experience during the two more years that he remained in the west. "At last," he wrote, "I found that living upon

fish, horses and roots would not do." Bankrupt in purse, but rich in experience he returned to a long career in the army.

1834

Nathaniel Wyeth, a Boston ice-dealer turned fur trader, made his second overland journey across the continent, and camped on the site of Boise. In his party were not only the first missionaries to the Far West–Jason Lee and his helpers–but also Thomas Nuttall, a botanist, and John H. Townsend, the famous ornithologist. On his return to the East, Townsend published a vivid account of his travels, and devoted several pages to a description of Boise Valley.

1836

The first white women who accomplished the arduous crossing of the continent from east to west were Mrs. Marcus Whitman and Mrs. Henry Spalding, who came with their husbands as missionaries to the Columbia River. The light wagon which they brought into the Boise Valley was the first wheeled vehicle that had ever come this far west. This feat marked the transition of the Oregon trail from a mere path into a highway.

1839

In this year the fur trade throughout the West reached its virtual end. In Boise Valley the fur-bearing animals had been trapped to extinction. Hundreds of mountain men, deprived of their livelihood, were turned adrift.

The departing bands of fur trappers had scarcely waved goodbye to their despoiled haunts before the roads leading west were choked with emigrants seeking home in the fertile valleys where the fur men had roamed. The first group that came with the avowed intention of settling in the Far West was the Farnham (or Peoria) party. They passed through Boise Valley, and although they observed its outstanding fertility, they did not consider it suitable for immediate settlement. Such was the perennial verdict as the intermittent tide of emigration flowed through Boise valley during the succeeding 25 years.

1843
After some 1,500 emigrants had already broadened and blazed the Oregon Trail by their passing, the Federal Government finally sent a military and scientific expedition under Lt. John C. Fremont to map the route and thereby make the Oregon journey easier for future colonists. Fremont was very pleasantly impressed by the Rivere Boisee, as also were the thousand emigrants who passed through Boise in this single year of the "Great Migration."

1845
Traffic along the Oregon Trail flourished as never before. Joel Palmer led a caravan of 37 wagons and subsequently published a guide-book, which not only encouraged hundreds of restless middle-western farmers to try their fortunes on the Pacific coast, but also gave them invaluable advice on the routes and methods of travel.

1848
In the treaty of this year, Great Britain renounced all her alleged or real rights to the Pacific Northwest between the 42nd and 49th parallels. Thus the Boise region became, for the first time, officially and definitely a part of the United States.

1849
A sudden cessation in the surge of emigration through Boise Valley occurred when news of the discovery of gold in California spread to the East. The vast majority of emigrants henceforward followed southwestward trails into the supposed California El Dorado, instead of following the older fur trail due west through Boise Valley.

1850-60
Because of the shift in migration, Boise Valley lapsed into aboriginal solitude broken only at intervals by the occasional passing of small groups of white-topped prairie schooners bound for the Oregon coast.

1854

During this vacant decade there took place on August 20, a few miles west of Boise, one of the worst tragedies that ever occurred on the Oregon Trail. A party of twenty-one emigrants led by Alexander Ward was ambushed by a far larger band of Snakes and massacred. Those not killed outright were hideously tortured and mangled. The only survivors were the two Ward boys, aged 13 and 15, who although badly wounded, managed to hide in the sagebrush. The younger boy was picked up by a rescue party, the older wandered over the desert for days before he reached Fort Boise.

Old Fort Boise (Courtesy of Boise State Special Collections and Archives)

1855

On July 18, almost 11 months to the day after the Ward massacre, three of the guilty Indians--all that had been caught--were marched by a detachment of U.S. troops to the site of the massacre and hanged upon gallows erected over the grave of the murdered victims. Although the gallows remained standing by the side of the wagon road for twenty years, this silent reminder did little to deter the same bands of Indians from assaulting and pillaging other wagon trains.

1860

Although Idaho's first gold fields, discovered in the northern part of the present state, attracted a population of thousands, only a minute fraction of them passed through Boise Valley, and none paused.

1862

In August, a party of prospectors led by George Grimes and Moses Splawn discovered that the mountain tributaries of Boise River were brimming with gold. Bannock Indians who had been dogging the prospectors' trail shot and killed Grimes shortly after the momentous discovery. The miners returned to Walla Walla for reinforcements and provisions, and arrived again in Boise Basin to found the camp of Pioneer. Before New Year's Day of 1863, four other roaring camps had been set up--Centerville, Placerville, Buena Vista, and Bannock City. Three thousand persons spent the winter in these camps preparing for the spring freshets, which were the prime necessity for carrying on placer operations.

1863

News of the gold discoveries in Boise Basin started a great rush of prospectors from California and Oregon in the early spring, even before the last snows had disappeared from the trail across the Blue Mountains. These hordes from the Coast did not pass through Boise Valley, but came into Boise from the north. The increasing contingents that came from Eastern points, particularly Colorado, entered the Basin by way of the Oregon Trail, and necessarily passed over the site of present Boise. Early in the spring Sherlock Bristol, a pioneer preacher, and a number of men broke a trail through the five feet of snow mantling the Boise Basin, and came into the Boise Valley where warm winds had melted the snow. They brought horses and cows to pasture on the lush valley grass, and took up claims. The sound of the axes and falling trees was heard everywhere, and huts and cabins began to spring up. One of these earliest settlers was I. N. Coston, who built a two story, drift-log cabin on the Boise River seven miles above Boise. This historic cabin has been moved to Julia Davis Park, and stands as a tangible memorial to Boise's earliest settlers.

Coston Cabin in Julia Davis Park (Courtesy of the Greater Boise Centennial Celebration Committee)

On March 3 Congress sliced off the eastern portion of gangling Washington Territory, added to it a far larger chunk of Dakotah Territory, and brought the mammoth result into legal existence as Idaho Territory. William Wallace of Washington Territory, appointed to the governorship by Abraham Lincoln chose as capital the "seaport" town of Lewiston. Lewistonians little dreamed in March 1863 that, far to the south, the half dozen log cabins on Boise River were destined to grow into a town influential enough, inside of 22 months, to wrest away the capital from its original site.

In May another party of men from the mountainous Boise Basin camps came down into the Boise Valley--not to settle, but to search for the supposedly lost mine known as the Blue Bucket Diggings. Passing through Boise Valley, they struck rich deposits on Jordan Creek, about sixty miles southward. A stampede followed and new mining towns sprang up like mushrooms. Thus Boise Valley became the cross-roads of gold trails from east to west, and north to south.

After urgent entreaties from the miners of the region, the War Department finally, in July, ordered a company of cavalry to Boise River, to build a garrison and subdue the marauding Indians who had become increasingly destructive. Arriving at Bristol's settlement, Major Lugenbeel established an army post, Boise Barracks. Three days later, Lugenbeel, Bristol and several enterprising merchants laid out the townsite of Boise. Immediately the new city became a trade center. The first merchants opened shops in the backs of their wagons, and soon made enough profit to erect sizeable buildings for conducting trade. Packstrings, blacksmiths, saloons, and stores carrying general merchandise located here and prospered.

Early view of the Boise barracks (Courtesy of Mark Baltes)

1864

Boise City was prospering and flourishing on its first birthday. A year before, land was free for the taking, but now fifty-foot residential lots sold for $150, twenty-five-foot business locations up to $1000.

On July 26, the *Idaho Statesman*, the third newspaper in Idaho, published its first issue (a tri-weekly sheet), in a log cabin at 6th and Main.

The Territorial Legislature cut a large slice out of Boise County, and set it up as a new county, named Ada. (After Ada Riggs, the first white child born here.) Boise was chosen as the county seat.

On December 7, Governor Caleb Lyon signed the legislative act removing the capital of the Territory from Lewiston to Boise. When Assemblyman Riggs returned to Boise from the legislative session, he was given a salute from the cannons at Fort Boise for his good work, but the people of Lewiston considered the transfer a dastardly deed.

1865

When the time came for the annual salmon run up the Boise River, citizens went out with pitchforks, only to be disappointed. Placer "tailings" and the waste from mining and milling had so contaminated the water that salmon were no longer able to exist, and what was once an abundant natural resource was lost to Boise forever.

Traffic through Boise on the Old Oregon Trail was so heavy that Main Street was often blocked for a half hour at a time. The townsmen gaped and stared at the ever-changing street scene. The local *Statesman* reported such items as the following: "The interesting sight, so familiar to California, of long trains of Celestials on the move, in single file, supporting the middle of their long handled shovels or a bamboo stock with pendant rice sacks, chopsticks, rockers and gum boots on their shoulders, filed along Idaho street yesterday morning to the great amusement of lookers-on. Some dusty pilgrims eyed the Johns with great curiosity, as it was their first introduction to the inhabitants of the Flowery Kingdom. John informed the curious crowd that he came from Washoe and was going to Bannock, from which we judge he is nearly as slow to learn the names and places in this country as some editors." Many of the industrious Orientals became wealthier than the scornful onlookers. Gold claims that the white owners thought were exhausted they sold to the Chinese, not discovering until afterward that most of the riches were still in the ground.

Central Hotel, 1888 (71-162-4. Courtesy of the Idaho State Archives)

Dr. Wright, a local druggist who lived to be 104 years old, was called upon to treat many cases of a strange new disease, seemingly indigenous to the sage and lava plains. This was the dreaded Rocky Mountain spotted fever, for which no certain cure has yet been developed.

Horace Gilson, Territorial Secretary, took charge of installing such equipment and records as had been laboriously brought down by pack train from the ex-capital, Lewiston. Gilson selected rooms in the old Central Hotel at 7th and Idaho, and these rented quarters were Boise's first Capitol Building.

1866

Horace Gilson, Territorial Secretary, having received from Washington, D.C. twenty-five thousand dollars in greenbacks to pay the expense of the legislative session, thereupon boarded a stagecoach going to the Pacific Coast, and was never heard from again. Some people thought he went to China. At any rate, the fat roll of greenbacks was never recovered.

The placer output began to subside. Mining was taken over by a few wealthy companies. At the same time there was an increasing interest in the agricultural development of the fertile land about the small city. Boise [would] soon be called the undisputed center of agriculture and trade.

Boise, 1866 (Courtesy of Boise Public Library)

By the spring of 1866, so many desperadoes from declining mining camps had drifted into the capital city in the hope of committing bigger and better paying crimes, that certain citizens organized the Boise City vigilance committee. The vigilantes were obliged to hang only two or three of the worst offenders, including the former sheriff, and all the rest departed quietly. The town was thus successfully cleared of its undesirable element.

Domestic tranquillity was upset by the Indians, who were desperately trying to maintain a last meagre foothold on their native soil. Soldiers from the Boise Barracks were called out in many small skirmishes. Townspeople were apprehensively alert whenever bands of Indians were reported in the vicinity.

1867

Boise city received its charter from the Territorial Legislature.

Governor Caleb Lyon (LC-BH82-4808 A. Courtesy of the Library of Congress)

Local papers quoted this item from a Washington, D.C. newspaper: "Yesterday Caleb Lyon of Lyonsdale, the governor of Idaho, arrived in this city and immediately went to police headquarters and said that on his way from New York he had a belt on his person containing $47,000, which he had safely carried all through the Rocky Mountains, California, and Idaho.

"This money consisted of ten $1000 bills and the rest in smaller bills which made it bulky. So he took it off and put it under his pillow in the sleeping car and on his waking in the morning found his belt at his feet without a dollar." To which news item and local *Statesman* snorted:

"This was the way he settled his accounts. Did anyone

ever hear such a fool story to cover up a clear defalcation? This did not go down and his bondsmen had to foot the bill. Doctor Swinburn, the health officer at the port of New York, was one of them and a worshipper of the old fool."

In June the First National Bank of Idaho, capitalized at $100,000, was opened. B. M. DuRell and C. W. Moore were partners in the firm. Their original office, one of the oldest buildings in the city, is now a grocery store.

The *Statesman* complained: "One can hear the most growling in Boise City about the detestable quality of stuff which is palmed off for 'fresh butter' than any other subject. If a man drinks bad whiskey or eats bad meat it is a voluntary thing with him; but in regard to butter it is a different affair. We must eat such as is set before us or go without. There is more bad butter to the 100 pounds sold by the ranchers to people in Boise City than any other place we ever saw--and we have lived in Oregon."

One Anthony McBride, an irascible citizen with a grudge against the red man became intoxicated, mistook a Chinese for an Indian, and shot him. As a result, McBride gained the honor of being the first murderer legally executed in Idaho.

1869

A territorial law library was established at Boise, books being purchased from fees paid by all lawyers admitted to the bar.

On Jan. 8 the entire town gathered at 7th and Idaho Streets to attend the unveiling of a gilded, life-size, equestrian statue of George Washington, which Charles Ostner, a Hungarian immigrant, hand carved, of native wood with common tools. A postage stamp was used as a model.

Charles Ostner with his statue of George Washington in its original location (74-155-0. Courtesy of the Idaho State Archives)

1870

On Independence Day the cornerstone of the new Territorial Penitentiary was laid. This small prison, 86 x 41 feet, was grimly and strongly built of rough-hewn Boise stone, and was the first structure in Idaho erected with federal funds. Construction work was slow, and Idaho's original population of two dozen were not brought down from the old wooden jail at Idaho City until March 1872.

Aerial view of the Idaho State Penitentiary, ca. 1915 (Courtesy of Mark Baltes)

The second edifice built with federal money was the U.S. Assay Office, 210 Main Street, at a cost of $83,000. It was begun in July, and officially opened a year later on March 2, 1872.

Assay Office (Courtesy of Mark Baltes)

1871
A new bridge across the Boise River, still in process of completion, was blown down by a heavy wind. The damage amounted to two thousand dollars.

1872

Boise City voted Republican for the first time in its history. At the same time, a newspaper was started, the *Idaho Democrat*. This became a bitter rival of the Republican *Statesman*, and many readers bought both papers to keep up with the verbal fight between editors.

1873

Statesman: "Templar Hall was crowded Tuesday evening to listen to Mr. McDougall's lecture on Temperance. The prisoner, a demijohn, was arraigned for all the crimes known to the criminal code and a strong case made against him. Mr. Barbour conducted the defense, and, although having everything against him, succeeded in making a very plausible plea for his client, though the verdict was rendered against him."

Statesman advertisement: "SWEDISH LEECHES: Just received at the Boise Drug Store."

1874
Traffic was often blocked and pedestrians endangered by the many cows and other barnyard beasts, which roamed at large in the streets, until an ordinance was passed prohibiting them from being loose.

1875
Jim Pinney, proprietor of the Boise City Book Store, was quoted as saying that the "fruitful condition of the county" had obligated him to make out an additional invoice of baby wagons.

1877
On Sept. 17, Boise was connected by telegraph with the outside world. The line was extended from Nevada through Silver City to reach the capital.

The Desert Land Act, passed by U.S. Congress, provided that anyone could acquire free title to as much as 640 acres by building the necessary irrigation works to water it. Bosie financiers were not slow in finding means to exploit this godsend.

Elite of the city were given the opportunity to enjoy the rare elocution of the Sawtelle Dramatic Company. The outstanding success of their melodramatic repertoire was entitled Driven From Home. Of another performance, the *Statesman* commented, "Mrs. Sawtelle gave readings from England's poet laureate so beautifully that many were raising their handkerchiefs surreptitiously to their eyes."

1878
William B. Morris of Boise constructed a six and a half-mile canal (later called the Ridenbaugh Canal), consequently acquiring, under the Desert Land Act,

Ridenbaugh Canal (75-40-3. Courtesy of the Idaho State Archives)

17,076 acres of land. The cost of his undertaking was only $60,000; yet within three years Morris had received $700,000 for the property.

Statesman (Feb. 5): At Professors Chapman and Hess's concert, "a novel and interesting feature of the performance will consist of the wonderful effects of the telephone. Turnverein Hall and Good Templar Hall will be connected by a wire, through which music and messages will be exchanged between them. All who witness this performance will be astonished and delighted."

Boundaries of Boise City were determined in a survey, and for the first time the exact city limits were learned. Stone corner posts marked these.

Statesman (April 11): "With all Boise City's braying about its Governor, it has not a fire engine yet."

The county commissioners allotted $38,225 to build a new brick courthouse for Ada County in the first block east of Capitol Square. Work began in August. The ornamental iron fence around the block cost $6000 alone.

1881

New silver quartz mines discovered in the Wood River region, northeast of Boise, brought such a flow of trade to Boise merchants that the *Statesman* editor, glancing at "main street, low-built and only a half dozen blocks long" prophesied: "If the business of Boise City increases next year in the same ratio as it has in the last two years not one of the five principal firms in this town will be able to do their business in a one-story building."

1882

Central School, an elegant two-story building, was completed. Both grade and high school classes were held in it until 1892.

Central School (Courtesy of Mark Baltes)

1883

During 1883, the rails were laid for the first transcontinental railway across Idaho. In spite of every effort that Boise could put forth, the railroad insisted on leaving the capital city off the main line--missing it by a mere dozen miles. The indignant but philosophical editor of the *Statesman* remarked: "This, however, is not our railroad, and the builders have a right to go where they please and will for ought we do or say. It is evident that railroads are built not to accommodate the people, but to accommodate the builders." Boise had to wait four full years before the Iron Horse actually came to the gates of the city--and even then it was but an inferior backtrack from an obscure station on the line.

1884

Statesman: "Many states and territories punish robbery with death. Our laws should do the same. Washington Territorial laws made highway robbery a capital offense. Our legislatures have overlooked the greatness of this crime, probably by copying from some other state statutes and have made it a state prison's offense. We hope to call attention of the legislature and ask to have the statutes changed."

The *New York Sun* regaled the effects East with a news item from the incredible wild west, regarding the arrival of Governor William M. Bunn: "Boise is the capital of Idaho. There's no capitol building as yet, the legislature sitting in a hall rented for the occasion. The Governor's executive office is a brick building only one story high. The new Governor arrived on the day of a circus, the Fourth of July. The proprietor proposed to suspend his morning performance and hold the gubernatorial celebration in the tent. His offer was accepted and the circus people joined in the procession. A platform was erected on one side of the ring, and on it sat eight ministers and a bishop. The tumblers, bareback riders, and acrobats waited until the close of the celebration; then the tent was cleared, the people bought tickets, and the show began."

Idaho Territorial Governor William Bunn (Public Domain, from *Some After Dinner Speeches* (1908))

1885

The Territorial Legislature passed a bill authorizing the construction of a Capitol building. Funds were provided by issuing $80,000 in 20-year bonds. E. E. Myers of Detroit was chosen architect, and he built a four-story brick structure which flamboyantly combined all the worst features of the typical warehouse and the typical "public building" of that era of bad taste. Nevertheless, it was acclaimed "the best building for the money west of the Missouri River." And at least it put an end to the exorbitant rents that had been paid annually to private landlords for inferior halls since 1865. The building was first used by the legislature on Dec. 13, 1886, on the occasion of the opening of the fourteenth session.

First Capitol building (Courtesy of Boise Public Library)

1887

Boise at last acquired a railroad connection when a branch line was extended from Nampa on the Oregon Short line, up the valley, to Boise. The depot, a crude board-and-batten shed, was located on the "bench" (the low foothills south of town). On Saturday, Sept. 5, the first official train chugged into the capital city. The *Statesman* was enthusiastic in a mild way: "On Sunday the road from town to the depot was lined with people nearly all day. The distance is about a mile, and the more fortunate ones rode in carriages, others in lumber wagons, and others on horseback, while hundreds of men, women and children walked over. It is safe to say that 1000 visited the railroad on Sunday."

First train depot (Courtesy of Boise Public Library)

Improvements began to come so fast they almost took people's breath away. Boise was provided with electricity, which rapidly began to replace flickering candles and smelly kerosene lamps.

The W.C.T.U. waged a noble war against public drunkenness. The results were immediate: in a single week two men were arrested and "taken to justice." Scoffers who declared that whiskey wasn't dangerous received a strong moral lesson when a wall of Arc Light Saloon collapsed, killing one man. The Salvation Army, decided that it's lone tamborine was insufficient to awaken sinners, so a fife and drum were added. Indeed, Boise's increasing modernity was bound to bring some bad results with all the good. There was [a] growing tendency to break the Sabbath. The *Statesman* piously remarked: "That baseball match for $300 takes place near the barracks on the sixteenth. The baseball is well enough, but we do not admire the idea of fixing the date for playing the game on Sunday."

The City Council passed an ordinance making it unlawful for mules to run across the bridges over Boise River.

1888
By 1888 the Territorial Legislature had appropriated more than twice as much money for the State Insane Asylum as for the State University.

1889
Territorial Governor George L. Shoup called a constitutional convention, which after a 26-day session, drew up a model constitution. At a special election the proposed constitution was ratified by a big popular majority.

Because of the constant increase in trade, growth in population, and the coming of the railroad, many new buildings were erected, the first three-story structure being the Brunbaum building at Eighth and Idaho streets.

1890
James Pinney built the Columbia Theatre in the southern half of Jefferson. The world-famous Julia Marlowe opened in *As You Like It*.

Joe Kinney's "Big Eddy Saloon" with its tripe, pickles,

bologna, mustard, and thickly sawdusted floor was for common people while Charles Granholm ran a high class place for real gentlemen only.

The Columbian Club, organized by the women of the capital city, took a leading part in civic improvements.

On July 3, Idaho was admitted as the forty-third state in the Union and Boise changed from a territorial to a state capital.

Columbia Theatre (Courtesy of Boise Public Library)

1891

In September the first electric street railway began operation.

A competition for selecting an appropriate design for the Great Seal of Idaho was announced by the Legislature. A young lady of Boise, Miss Emma Edwards, submitted the winning design.

1892

The natatorium building, supplied with natural hot water, was constructed to enclose the second largest indoor swimming pool in the world. The building itself was of Moorish architecture, three stories high, with two great towers in front. In addition to the pool, there were dining halls, billiard rooms, and floors for dancing.

1894

St. Alphonsus hospital was established by five Sisters of the Holy Cross.

Troops were sent from the Boise Barracks to arrest part of Coxey's Army marching through Pocatello.

Under the Carey Act, passed by the United States Congress, Idaho gained a million acres to be reclaimed by irrigation. Irrigation farming was rapidly becoming the mainety of Boise's economic life.

The *Statesman* made a scoop on the following news item: "Churches Plan Crusade against Vice When Weather Cools. The church people of the city will, it is said, shortly commence the most vigorous and relentless war upon sin that has ever been inaugurated in Idaho's capital. It is understood that as soon as the weather moderates, revivals are to commence in all the leading churches, and the industrious individual who is said to preside over a locality even hotter than this, will be vanquished ignominiously if it be within the power

Irrigation ditch (Courtesy of Mark Baltes)

of those who wage this crusade against the immoral ones to do so. The crusaders will insist that disreputable dives of all kinds be closed, or at least removed from the prominent positions they now occupy."

St. Alphonsus Hospital (Courtesy of Mark Baltes)

1896

Second amendment of Idaho's constitution adopted at legislative session in Boise. This extended to women equal rights of suffrage, Idaho being the third state in the Union to pass such a law.

1897

First women jurors to serve in Idaho were empaneled in a case at Boise.

William E. Borah, Boise lawyer, was elected to the United States Senate. Borah, by some, was considered an eastern tenderfoot. But citizens in general liked the young attorney, and he was elected on the first ballot by an overwhelming majority.

Senator William Borah, 1922 (LC-H234- A-4851. Courtesy of the Library of Congress)

The city council placed Boise City on mountain time which is forty- five minutes behind the time used by the railroad.

1898

Bowlers, bustles, and bicycles became Boise Fashion. Boise Bicycle Club staged a beautiful parade and a big bicycle meet. Prizes were presented for the prettiest bicycle floats. To the winner of the meet went a gold medal, the man taking second place received all the soda pop he could drink in August, and the honor of third place merited a handsome bicycle bell.

An attempt was made to keep Flaming Youth of the gay nineties under control, as this news item indicates: "The curfew ordinance was enforced last night for the first time. The school bell was rung at eight o'clock as a warning to all children that it was time to be home. After the bell sounded, all persons under sixteen years of age must be indoors or be subject to arrest. Chief Francis says in case of public entertainment, when children go immediately home after they are over, no arrests will be made. Therefore the gallery god at the theatre will continue to occupy his customary place and regale the audience with the latest thing in cat calls."

At the turn of the century, the modern mania for speed began to develop, and the local transportation companies were prompt to satisfy their patrons, especially when coming down from the mountaintop mining camps into Boise. The *Statesman* for July 3 gave the latest news on speeding up travel: "The rival stage companies enjoyed something of a race coming out of Silver City yesterday. The Boggs stage overtook the Boomer stage at Breshears, where the latter stopped for Breakfast, and the Boomer stage passed the opposition about nine miles from Guffey. The Boggs stage lost a wheel and was about two hours later getting in. The passengers were jammed, scratched, and bruised, but none of them were seriously injured."

Statesman advertisement: "Souvenir Spoons Given Away. 'Remember the Maine' spoons given with each ten cent purchase of chewing gum. Joy's Drug Store."

1902

A big year of expansion. The amount of money spent on new buildings was over a million dollars, about two dollars a minute. Wholesale business showed a 25 percent increase over the previous year, express receipts doubled those of 1901. There were seventy-nine new business concerns established. A new high school building was begun at Tenth and Washington streets, and St. Teresa's Academy for girls was erected at Third and Jefferson. The first National Bank Building at Eighth and Main, and the Gem Block at Tenth and Main, were now downtown structures.

First National Bank, at far left, at Eighth and Main Streets, ca. 1904 (82-13-3. Courtesy of the Idaho State Archives)

1903

Big excitement was caused by the arrival of a New York capitalist driving a $3,500 automobile, described in the *Statesman* as "The largest and most complete ever brought to the city, one of those long drawn-out affairs often seen in the East but never before in this section." He found it difficult to store this elegant machine, for all the liverymen in town were both afraid of it and feared for its safety.

Central fire station was constructed.

Central Fire Station, 1904 (William F. "Doc" Roach Collection. Courtesy of Boise State Special Collections and Archives)

1904

An announcement appearing in the *Statesman* for June 3 revealed the new age of chivalry in Boise. "The Boise Baseball Association has decided to admit ladies to the grounds and grandstand free of charge on Wednesdays and Fridays. To induce a man to cease smoking in the grandstand so as not to offend the ladies is not an easy task and the club officials do not wish to be too arbitrary. The 'No Smoking' rule was well observed yesterday and it is predicted that all smokers will have become accustomed to going to the bleachers for their smoking."

The first automobile hack service was started. The announcement stated that one car was in operation and another would be put on as soon as business would justify it. A "thoroughly experienced chauffeur" was in charge.

The venerable Methodist Church building was leased and fitted up as the "Star" vaudeville house.

Main and Idaho streets were paved with asphalt paving at cost of $180,000 and ten alleys were paved with bricks.

1905

The State Supreme Court helped to emancipate women by declaring unconstitutional law which, under penalty of a severe fine, forbade women to enter saloons.

Carnegie Public Library, a $23,000 structure, was dedicated and opened to the public on Thursday, June 22. It was erected on the site of Boise's first tax-supported school, which was sold to the highest bidder for $55 and moved away to make room for the library. This historic, one-room, red brick building, under whose roof many of the pioneers and prominent citizens of the town had gained their education, had long since been abandoned for school purposes and had been converted into a carriage painting shop.

Carnegie Public Library architectural rendering by J. E. Tourtellotte & Co. (Charles Frederick Hummel Papers. Courtesy of Boise State Special Collections and Archives)

On May 27, Boise was visited by one of the worst floods in its history. Two cloudbursts in the hills north of the city caused the flood. The first occurred about 7:30 P.M. and roared down Kelly Hot Springs Gulch. The second occurred about 8:45 when Cottonwood Creek overflowed and swept like a wall toward the city. About 10 o'clock the tide of water reached Boise Barracks, hurled itself through the military reservation with mighty force, and out a channel to the head of Fifth Street, where the waters were temporarily abated by pouring into the Perrault Ditch. When this overflowed, nearly every street leading south was converted into a torrent of muddy water, and practically the entire city south of the Fort, from eastern limits to the western, was submerged. The water fairly leaped into Fort street and rushed toward the business district. When it reached the paved section, it gained speed. At the corner of Eight and Main, the heart of the commercial district, the sidewalks were soon lost to sight. Many persons returning from places of amusement were marooned. At one place on Main street several women climbed onto a picket fence and were forced to remain there over an hour before they could be rescued. The wholesale district was spared by the fact that the Grove street ditch caught the remainder of the thinning tide. By 3 A.M. the flood had commenced to subside.

For the first time in the history of the city, saloons were

required to lock up at midnight. Practically none of the saloons had ever closed their doors before (except theoretically on election day), and some of them found that their doors had no locks. Locksmiths had a busy time on the day that the new ordinance went into effect.

During the hot summer months, local Prohibitionists placed cold water barrels on the several street corners for the benefits of thirsty customers. W.C.T.U women "coyly tried to make their principles seem agreeable" by purchasing ice for the barrels.

1906

Local newspaper rejoiced in the coming of the machine age: "Mr. J. E. Clinton, Jr., is the latest auto enthusiast to procure a new machine, his splendid motor car arriving on Thursday. The number of machines increasing rapidly now, and the smell of gasoline along the countryside is lending an air of refinement to the whole valley. There is talk of organizing an automobile club in the near future."

The Warden of the State Penitentiary at Boise announced that Idaho had a prison population of seventy-five. Five more prisoners, he warned, would cause the prisons to be overcrowded.

Entrance to the Idaho State Penitentiary (Courtesy of the Boise Department of Arts & History)

The capital city was host to the National Irrigation Congress. At this convention, plans were laid to induce Congress to allot a hundred million dollars for irrigation projects. Boise Valley profited immeasurably from the federal irrigation works that were subsequently begun.

For the first time in the city's 43 years of existence, Boise was able to boast of a park for recreational purposes. The local streetcar company enhanced the interurban line by establishing a pleasant park several miles outside the city limits. It had an artificial lake, with launches and rowboats. A natural meadow thickly set with native poplar and willow trees provided a restful setting for Sunday excursions.

Catholics celebrated the erection of St. John's cathedral, an imposing structure of rough ashlar sandstone, replacing the rambling wooden church that had served since pioneer days. After thirty years, the two spires of the facade are still uncompleted.

This winter Boise suffered from a shortage of coal, caused by labor troubles in the East. The small amount of coal mined did not find its way across the Rockies. Local supplies of dry wood were at a premium, and green timber had to be hauled over many miles of snowbound mountain roads. This caused at least one Boise firm to be strong in the market for sagebrush, which could be obtained in abundance within eight miles of Boise. Properly trimmed, it made good fuel, and sold for more than $6 a cord.

Local papers pointed to the glorious possibilities of Boise Valley and its diversity in a news account of two neighboring farmers, one of whom was engaged in cutting eight inch slabs of ice from his farm pond at the same time that his neighbor was sowing winter rye in loose dry soil of a new field. The latter farmer explained that the field in which he was drilling the rye was now sagebrush land that had never been irrigated and that it was so dry it could not freeze, though irrigated land in adjacent fields were frozen hard.

December 31: Assassination of ex-Governor Steunenberg.

Governor Frank Steunenberg, 1900 (66-16-1. Courtesy of the Idaho State Archives.)

1907

While Senator William E. Borah was reaping worldwide fame in the Haywood trial, he was indicted by a grand jury on a charge of conspiracy to defraud the government of valuable timber lands in Boise Basin. He was, however, acquitted on October 2, 1907. "The announcement of the verdict was heard by probably the largest crowd of spectators that ever jammed and crowded into the federal courtroom, and the reading of the verdict was greeted by a tremendous demonstration, shouts of triumph, clapping of hands, stomping of feet and waving of arms. It was exactly 6 o'clock when word was passed from the federal building. A second later the fire bell sounded and the bell beat its tattoo while the firemen aboard their equipment dashed down the street. This was the signal for the gathering. The news spread like wildfire over the city and crowds gathered on Main street. The Columbian band was summoned and led the shouting crowd. Senator Borah and his chief counsel, James H. Hawley, were rushed from the federal building to the hotel and amid ringing cheers of happy throngs were escorted to the Idanha balcony. Mr. Hawley made a brief speech, followed by the senator."

Electric street car looking south on Eighth Street, with Boise City Hall on the left and the Chamber of Commerce on the right (Courtesy of Mark Baltes)

In February the first transportation within the city by electric street cars was begun. The system consisted at first of only about one mile of rails, and was a ten-minute ride.

On November 22, the city council officially accepted from Thomas Davis, one of Boise's pioneers, a fine tract of 40 acres lying directly south of the city on the north bank of Boise River. As Julia Davis Park, this gradually became one of the greatest assets of Boise the beautiful.

Boise boasted of having three women serving as rural mail carriers. They were said to be the only women so employed in the United States.

The County Courthouse was crowded to capacity when Harry Orchard, confessed dynamiter, told in horrible detail how he had prepared his homemade bomb and placed it at the gate of ex-Governor Steunenburg's residence. Two thirds of the spectators at the trial were women.

"Big Bill" Haywood was acquitted by the jury of a charge of murdering Steunenberg. He shook hands with each juryman and his lawyers. Much excitement was manifested in all the public places of Boise.

State Historical Society and Museum was established by the State Legislature and given rooms in the Capitol building.

State Legislature passed a severe Sunday blue law; the Sabbath was declared a day of public rest, and all places of business and amusement were closed on that mournful day.

First Ada County Courthouse (Courtesy of Mark Baltes)

1908

1908 was one of Boise's sunniest years--both literally and metaphorically. According to the weather bureau, the sun shone during no fewer than 353 days throughout the year. Other statistics showed that Boise did more business than any city of the same in the United States and that Boise had fewer mortgages than any city of its size in the West. Three-quarters of a million dollars were expended on the construction of new buildings.

1909

Increasing indications of the machine age were noted in a newspaper item: "The year 1909 will see the automobile introduced to more Boise citizens than ever before. We have 45 cars. E. H. Beggs is bringing into town the fine Stanley Steamer. It makers claim that it will travel 127 miles per hour, and has no rival for hill climbing either. Randall and Dodd are exhibiting the Buick and Thomas cars. The farmers are looking into their usefulness and buying them up. On the coast, even women are driving cars, and soon Boise women will be seen in the driver's seat."

1910

During 1910 probably more changes were wrought in appearance of Boise's business building district then in any year before or since. Dozens of antique wooden buildings disappeared. $1,300,000 was expended in the construction of at least 40 new buildings. Among those were three six-story structures, which still remain the tallest and largest landmarks of the skyline, with the single exception of a twelve-story hotel built in 1930. In this flurry of construction was included what Boise proudly pointed to as the largest moving picture theatre in the world. One of the massive six-story [buildings was] also hailed as the largest building in Idaho.

1912

The forest of telephone poles, with their overhead maze of electric wires, disappeared during the course of this year from the main streets, all electric wires being laid underground. Old photographs show that the telephone poles were quite a problem in their day. Inasmuch as they were used for hitching posts along the street, the lower portion of each pole had to be coated with tar, and wound with barb-wire, in order to keep hungry horses from making a meal out of them.

The steady rise in property value caused many taxpayers to complain. Lots increased in market value almost 100% in 3 years. The tax rate remaining the same, landowners were forced to pay a 100% increased levy.

1913

On May 5, the settled district south of the Boise River was annexed, and became part of Boise. The consolidation made it necessary to rename 20 streets, as there were that many duplications.

The northwest end of the city was swept by a torrent, July 25. A cloudburst, rushing down Hull's Gulch, flooded the residential section. Lawns were ruined, cellars inundated, and muddy debris left everywhere.

1914

Boise enjoyed great prosperity during 1914. Much of this was due to the activity of the Boise-Payette Lumber Co. whose mill, a few miles from the city, provided the city's largest industrial payroll. The lumber company constructed a million-dollar railroad into the Boise Basin where the chief reserves of timber were located. Optimistic hopes that Boise would become the "center of a monumental lumber industry" did not, however, come to realization.

1916

On January 1st, Idaho became a dry state without waiting for Mr. Volstead's sanctions. Boise, veneered with respectability, abstained from commotion in signaling the exit of demon rum. With the stroke of the New Year "the Barley-corn family took their departure with no disorder and little hilarity. Nobody smiled and there were no farewell drinks. Some of the bars closed early in the evening when they ran out of stock. The slot machines were heavily played as they, too, were going out of business. The town just went dry by degrees, and that's all there was to it. On the stroke of the hour, the beer taps were opened and bottles were emptied into the sink."

1917

Local newspapers reported that Boiseans were aghast at declaration of war. Idaho National Guard, 600 strong, mobilized at Fort Boise on the day of declaration. The Barracks assumed a military appearance such as it had not manifested for many years.

1918

On November 11, at 4 A.M. (Idaho time) the world war ended. Boise leaped into motion; crowds gathered with noise making instruments; the bells of the city were rung. The noise of rejoicing continued throughout the early morning hours.

1919

The first Music Week in the U.S. was originated by the Boise Civic Festival Chorus, and the first presentation took place the week of May 11-16. Since then it has been an annual event, attracting musicians and spectators from the entire state. Scores of cities throughout the country have subsequently initiated a yearly festival of music, patterned after Boise's model.

School pageant for Music Week, 1935 (Courtesy of Boise Music Week)

A bloodless revolution in the state capital completely changed Idaho's system of government. April 4th was the epochal day on which 81 tangled bureaus and boards with separate officers but overlapping duties, were reorganized into nine departments. At the head of each department the Governor appointed a commissioner. This inaugurated the cabinet form of administration, which has persisted through 20 mixed years of praise and criticism.

Two landmarks were torn down to make room to add the wings to the central portion of the capitol. One was the venerable Central School, which had stood on Capitol Square since 1882. The other was the old Capitol building (designated as the Capitol Annex since 1912), said to be one of the last two remaining brick statehouses in the United States.

1921

Perhaps no other section of the U.S. bore the brunt of the post-war high cost of living so heavily as did Idaho, whose inaccessible location gave profiteers a glorious chance to extort heinous transportation charges from the consumer. The cost of government was another burden that weighed oppressively on everyone, not only through explicit taxation but even more through the invisible taxes that were added to selling prices. The predominantly rural legislature who came to the Capitol seemed unable to cope with the financial bogeys of the day, and this invoked more than one revealing editorial, such as the following: "It seems like a great mistake to bring our lawmakers here from the modest surroundings which we of Idaho all live, and place them in marble halls, with mahogany desks and mosaic floors, among luxurious appointments of every kind, and then try to get them to realize we are broke. They should remember that our imitation jewelry has been purchased on the installment plan--$420 an hour as long as you live. Dear lawmakers, forget the marble. It is a concrete proposition that must be met."

During a period when a radio was still clumsily called a "wireless receiving apparatus," Boise enthusiasts established a sending and receiving station, 7-Y-A, in conjunction with the high school science curriculum.

1922

The noteworthy event of the year was the visit of a Chicago millionaire to Boise. He dispenses lofty advice to local yokels: "If the farmers of Idaho would go about teaching the other citizens how to consume their products, instead of dabbling in politics and trying to improve conditions that way, their own condition would be improved much more quickly." As far as could be observed, the farmers kept dabbling.

1923
Among Boise's 24,000 inhabitants, the city welfare director found 24 families on the relief list. Most of these, she claimed, were on public charity because of "lazy husbands." Worst of all was the moral depravity of these unfortunates, as indicated by the fact that only one person expressed thanks for the aid given at Christmas time.

1925
Boise at last succeeded in getting placed on a transcontinental railroad, after enduring for 37 years the tribulations of being on a cumbersome spur line. More than fifteen thousand visitors, straining all hotel and restaurant facilities, jammed the city to take part in the mammoth celebration on April 16th. Never before had Boise witnessed such lavish

festivities, and nothing equal in grandeur can be anticipated for the future. The new depot, of California-Spanish architecture, is magnificently located on the brow of the mesa so as to overlook a broad tract of tree-filled Boise Valley.

Aerial view of the "new" train depot (Courtesy of Mark Baltes)

1926

During the early part of this year, a municipal airport was established and a hanger built. On April 6th, a celebration was held to inaugurate the placing of Boise on a federal airmail route.

Boise Municipal Airport (AR 020390. Courtesy of Boise State Special Collections and Archives)

By construction of Sunset Drive, a new rapid route was opened leading into the pine-clad hills, serving as Boise's skyline on the north, which had always hitherto been inaccessible for auto travel. This 12 mile scenic drive, terminating in a natural playground area, was built by a local civic club.

1927
Among the hundred-odd items ground through the 19th State Legislature, there was perhaps none more characteristic of Idaho's pioneer, close-to-the-soil spirit than the bill which declared chicken stealing a felony, and gave farmers the right to shoot upon sight the perpetrator of such felony.

1929

Upon the eve of the Great Depression no one in Boise suspected its advent. On the contrary, western optimism never reigned more rampantly. One million dollars was expended for building operations during 1929, the downtown lighting system was modernized, the city park was extended and improved, and the water company was obligated to tear out the rotting wooden water mains and replace them with cast iron mains. With bank clearings seven million dollars greater than 1928, the only real handicap to happiness was the difficulty of procuring non-poisonous brands of choice "imported" liquors.

1930

Again in 1930, one million dollars was invested in construction work, of which about a third was spent on the Hotel Boise, at present the city's most conspicuous and graceful building. Governor Baldridge declared that Idaho's economic structure was "ready to sustain any conceivable shock." As winter drew on, the unemployment problem began to loom up. Nevertheless, Boise was among the last cities of the nation to feel the oncoming depression.

Idaho's isolations from national problems and incredulity at the persistence of hard times, were well revealed when a local newspaper discovered the surprising fact that many men were out of work. The newspaper item concluded with naive candor: "Never has there been such a run of penniless fellows around Boise."

One of the chief attractions of the city was created by the widening of Capitol Boulevard, providing a straight approach from the depot on the hill down through the heart of the city to the door of the Capitol Building. The boulevard crosses the Boise River near the spot where hundreds of emigrants forded the river in pioneer days to enter the city; and a handsome concrete bridge designated as the Oregon Trail Memorial Bridge was built as part of the boulevard project.

Oregon Trail Memorial Bridge (Courtesy of the Boise Department of Arts & History)

1932

While certain Boise groups, hoping to bring about the repeal of stringent prohibition laws, flaunted such slogans as, Save American Youth from Menace of Poisonous Bootleg Booze, the local police seized stills of the illicit liquor whenever complaints made it expedient to enforce the law. A newspaper in reviewing the year's contraband, warmed statistical: "If all the rum confiscated by Boise police in a year were put into a huge receptacle, it would float a yacht--well, at least a rowboat."

In spite of lower city taxes, and a lower total income, the city made many municipal improvements, including construction of Fairview Bridge, oiling of 22 miles of streets, and dredging and straightening the river.

1933

The November general elections, at which Idaho citizens voted (overwhelmingly) to end the 18-year reign of Volstead, gave the state legislature authority to draft proper laws to control the scale and distribution of liquor. However, the citizenry could not wait for the legislature to give its ceremonious legislation to an ancient ritual, so several Idaho towns proceeded to pass local ordinances defining beer as non-intoxicating (though this was contrary to state law). The governor was obligated to call the state legislature into special session in June in order to settle the beer problem. On and after June 21, beer with less than 3.2% alcohol was defined as non-intoxicating [and] became a legal product. Later the legislature dealt with hard liquor by banning saloons and establishing a system of state dispensaries under control of a State Liquor Commision. Boiseans endeavored to readjust themselves to legal drinking.

Looking back on the long pre-repeal era, it was agreed that, after all, prohibition had been better than having the city plumb dry.

On September 28, an auditor delving into the city treasurer's books uncovered evidence of the great embezzlement that had occurred since the days of the late 60's when the Boise Vigilance committee worked to suppress dishonest office holders. Arrest of the treasurer, daughter of a respected pioneer family, followed. On October 24 she plead guilty and was transferred the same day to the state prison to begin serving a 1-to-10 year sentence. The speculations, extending over a period of 10 years, were first estimated at $10,000, but were later discovered to aggregate more than $50,000.

1935
Governor C. Ben Ross began his third consecutive term in office, and thereby established a precedent, as no previous Idaho governor had ever had three terms.

Boise was flooded with sunshine in 1935, according to annual weather report. The sun shed its beams upon the city for a daily average of 8 hours, 8 1/2 minutes.

1936
Arrowrock Dam, the source of Boise Valley irrigation wealth, was further enhanced in value when an extra five feet in height was added to the dam at an expenditure of $294,000.

1937
After many years of fruitless complaints against inadequacy of the ancient County Courthouse, at last Ada County voters put up a bond issue, which, with federal help, will build a respectable, modern seven-story courthouse.

Arrowrock Dam (Albert E. Nelson Photographs. Courtesy of Boise State Special Collections and Archives)

New Ada County Courthouse (Courtesy of Mark Baltes)

Capitol Boulevard looking north (Courtesy of Mark Baltes)

Part III: Points of Interest

For the visitor, especially from the East where grandeur in public edifices is a commonplace, Boise has little to offer in points of interest except those items which still endure as monuments to the spirit of the early West.

The State Capitol

Standing at the northern end of Capital Boulevard and facing at the far southern end the Howard Platt Gardens and the Union Pacific station is by far the most impressive structure in the city and is clearly visible from all points of approach. Designed by Tourtellotte and Hummel of Boise, it is architecturally similar to the Capitol in Washington, D. C., St. Peter's Cathedral in Rome, St. Paul's Cathedral in London, and all other edifices which have a "vaulted dome patterned after the canopy of Heaven."

Begun in 1905 and completed (east and west wings) in 1920, the building is chiefly of Boise sandstone, with the lower story motif representing the log cabin era. The cost, including grounds and furnishings, was $2,229,338.15. The cubic content is 4,377,897 feet. The dimensions, not including approaches, are 398 feet in length and 224 in depth. The height to the top of the dome is 195 feet. The area covered by the capitol and approaches is 50,646 square feet.

The interior is finished in Vermont, Italian and Alaskan marble. The great dome is supported (and in this respect is said to be unique) by huge steel columns 5 feet in diameter and 60 feet in height, faced with marble. These columns, Corinthian in design, have beautiful capitals. On the second floor are the offices of several state departments; on the third floor are the Supreme Court chambers, the law library, and the House and Senate chambers in the wings. From the dome, admission to which is free, is afforded a view of the city and the valley.

There is not a great deal of interest in the Capitol. Notably on the second floor in the rotunda is a statue of George Washington mounted on a horse. This statue was carved by Charles N. Ostner from native white pine many years ago. He used a postage stamp for the model of the face. In the basement is the State Historical Society.

Idaho State Capitol at night (Charles Frederick Hummel Papers. Courtesy of Boise State Special Collections and Archives)

Among the items of greatest interest to visitors in the State Historical Society (open 9-5, admission is free) are several excellent collections of Indian artifacts; various relics of pioneer life, including a stage coach, implements and tools, guns and household furniture; a few souvenirs relating to the Reverend Spalding's missionary work among the Indians; the prehistoric bones of animals uncovered in the Hagerman Valley area by expeditions from the Smithsonian's institute, including the skeleton of a very rare species of ancient horse; the interesting miniature of the Sandpoint Bridge, a wooden structure two miles long; the files of old newspapers crammed with the lore of a time that is dead; and

Idaho State Historical Society in the basement of the Capitol, 1924 (598c. Courtesy of the Idaho State Archives)

assortments of semi precious or curious stones and of various types of petrified wood.

The foregoing are only a few of the thousands of items that have been collected. Persons accustomed to the contents of historical societies often turn away to gaze with rapt interest at the photographs of bearded worthies who look down from the walls; for here is one of the most fascinating collections to be found in the West of fashions in whiskers.

Union Pacific Station

Until 1925, Boise was not on the main line of a railroad; and when growth of the city made a change mandatory, it was decided not only that the line must not run through the city, but also that the new station must be one of surpassing beauty. By building 25 1/2 miles of new line from Orchard to Boise, and by using a part of the old Nampa branch, Boise was placed upon the great artery of the Union Pacific System.

The Union Pacific station at the southern end of Capital Boulevard is said to be one of the most beautiful in the country. Built at a cost of $240,000 exclusive of landscaping, and designed by Carrere and Hastings of New York City, it is architecturally a modified type of early Spanish. It is constructed of brick without stone trim. The exposed brick being plastered to give a stucco appearance. An outstanding feature is the clock tower which rises to a height of 110 feet, and in which is housed a set of beautiful chimes.

Boise Depot
(Courtesy of
Mark Baltes)

 Because persons journeying though are often depressed by the arid terrain eastward, it was decided to landscape the grounds, and to allow a stop of ten or fifteen minutes in Boise so that weary passengers could gaze at the Howard Platt gardens and be refreshed. These, covering a little more than three acres, were designed by Ricardo Espino, Los Angeles architect. Here are no ugly yards and sheds, but a grotto, cascading water, terraces and pools. The walks are bordered with rambling roses, petunias and phlox. Norway maples, blossoming catalpas and several weeping willows are upon the grounds. At night, searchlights make sorcerous loveliness of the gardens.

Julia Davis Park

Boise's park system began twenty years ago when Thomas Davis gave the city 45 acres of land along the north bank of Boise River, and asked that the park be named Julia Davis in memory of his deceased wife. With gifts or purchases since then, the area has been increased to about ninety acres, and will be, when finally landscaped and completed, one of the largest parks in the intermountain country.

Lagoon inside Julia Davis Park (Courtesy of Mark Baltes)

Julia Davis Park lies just east of Capitol Boulevard and just north of Boise River. In recreation facilities it offers tennis courts, a children's playground, a long lagoon and boating, a wide variety of shrub and tree and lovely picnic spots. Of principal interest to visitors are the Coston and Agnew-Pierce cabins, two of the earliest Boise homes. Both were erected in 1863, and both are typical of early pioneer homes in this area. In them are a few pioneer relics but admission, though free, is by appointment only with the park superintendent.

Alligator fountain, Julia Davis Park (Courtesy of Frank Aden Jr.)

The park has a very small zoo which was begun in 1916 when a monkey who escaped from a passing circus was captured out in the sagebrush and penned. Today there are forty species of animal and bird. Of greatest interest to outsiders are the cougar, coyote, elk and deer, the western red-tail hawks, and golden eagles. Outside the zoo, on the lagoon, are a great many wild ducks and geese, some of which are so tame that they will approach to be fed. The park area is a wild bird preserve, and thousands of transient water fowl visit the waters of the park or the river flowing upon the southern boundary.

Deer reserve, Julia Davis Park (Courtesy of Mark Baltes)

O'Farrell Cabin

On Fort street north and a little east of the Capitol, this historic pioneer cabin (some say the first, and in any case one of the first built on the present site of Boise) was constructed by John A. O'Farrell in the fall of 1863. It was originally on the lot at 418 Franklin St. In those early days it was regarded almost as a palatial home, especially after other rooms had been added and the outside covered with adobe. Fireplace and flue were built of bricks made at the fort nearby. The floor was originally of clay, but later of boards which still record the tramping of hobnailed boots.

O'Farrell Cabin
(Courtesy of
Mark Baltes)

When the cabin was moved in 1912 to its present site, it was given a new roof of shakes, made from blocks of cedar with a drawing-knife, as the original ones had been. Everything else about the cabin remains unaltered. A pewter tea kettle and brass bucket swing from the hooks of the fireplace. Above the doorway is a bronze tablet declaring that this was the first home in Boise to shelter women and children. It also seems probable that the first church services in Boise were held in this historic structure.

DeLamar House

This historic structure, standing at the corner of 8th and Grove and serves now as a Basque rooming-house, is almost lost in legend. It is called the DeLamar house because one of the most picturesque characters in early Idaho history the Belgian Colonel (or Captain, and perhaps in actual fact neither) DeLamar bought it after he had made millions out of mining in Owyhee County. The Colonel, it seems, felt that it was necessary, after accumulating vast wealth, to establish himself in a home that fitly symbolized his aspirations. That he built the house, as legend often declares, seems not to be a fact.

The house was built by C. W. Moore, the first cashier of the first National Bank of Boise. In its day [it] was a noble, even if according to present taste ornate, structure on the most exclusive street in the city. Since its erection it has changed hands many times. DeLamar apparently tired of it soon, for he rented it to the Arid Club of Boise for a clubhouse. It was subsequently owned by W. E. Peirce, pioneer Boise real estate dealer; and became in turn the home of W. E. Borah, famous Idaho senator; and then the home of Mateo Arregui who finally sold it to Adriana Arregui in whose possession today it serves as a rooming-house.

DeLamar house turned hotel (1242-D. Courtesy of the Idaho State Archives)

Bohemian Breweries

The plant of the Bohemian Breweries is at 111 N. 6th. (Visitors are welcomed.) There are of course, much larger breweries in the country; but the making of beer is the same in any of them, and the making of beer is much more fascinating procedure than anyone who contemplates so simple a product would be likely to suppose. Briefly, step by step, it is as follows.

First, there is the warehouse full of bags of Idaho malted barley. The grain is shipped to Spokane for malting where it is soaked and allowed to sprout. Machines thereupon knock off the sprouts and the grain is sacked and returned. In the Bohemian plant it is then crushed and poured into the huge mast vats within which whirling machinery keeps it busy. At the bottom of these vats are spouts through which the extract is released and delivered to a second series of containers, floored with large copper coils, in which it is boiled. From here the liquid flows to a third series of vats and the hops are strained out; and is then pumped upstairs into enormous wooden receptacles. It is here mixed with yeast and the fermentation begins--and of most appetizing variety and bouquet are the odors in this huge room.

After fermenting, the liquid is piped to other gigantic vats where, kept at an even temperature, fermentation continues. It then goes to aging vats in the cellar downstairs where it remains for two months; and is removed then to the final huge drums where it is filtered and carbonated and bottled. These are great pressure tanks. Out of them the beer flows through a government tax meter which registers every drop; because no beer can be made upon which Uncle Sam does not get his revenue.

In the Bohemian plant there are usually 7,000 barrels in the process of aging. After the beer has grown into approved fragrance and flavor, it is driven under enormous pressure into kegs and bottles; whereupon the bottled product is pasteurized under heat. Because pasteurization changes the flavor a little, some retailers demand draught beer which is unpasteurized. Pasteurized beer will keep indefinitely under any temperature; but the other has to be kept cold.

Nothing is more likely to impress the visitor then the elaborate measures taken to ensure cleanliness. Several times daily, all the machinery, hoses and preliminary receptacles are cleaned under hot steam pressure; and the returned bottles and kegs are subjected to hot steam baths and to almost microscopic examination. The brew-meister declares that for most persons, cleanliness is certainly not next to godliness; because among the persons employed not more than two out of every ten are able to learn how to fastidiously clean everything in the making of beer.

Bohemian Brewery, 1961 (63-176-72. Courtesy of the Idaho State Archives)

Bird's eye kite view looking east (Courtesy of Mark Baltes)

Part IV: Tours in Environs

Tour 1
Boise---Table Rock and Return
About 5 miles

From the Capitol Building the route goes North on Eighth street to Fort street and then on Fort to the first street running east of the Boise Barracks. It follows this street northward to the foothills and swings to the right and up over the foothills and follows a meandering course. Table Rock will be clearly visible in the east from nearly all points of the road and the course cannot very well be missed.

CAUTION: Locally, this is known as the Skyline Drive and is [safe] for experienced drivers. Drivers not at ease on moderately difficult mountain road should not attempt it.

Tablerock, said to have been a lookout point and council ground of Indians in early times, affords an excellent view of Boise and Boise Valley, and is very popular as a vantage point, especially at sunset and after dark. The great mountain upon which the flat table rests is much more than an ordinary mountain. It is a huge deposit of sandstone of a quality which has, in times past, been in national demand. Structures in Boise made of this excellent stone include the Capitol, the Art Gallery, and the Federal Building. Structures elsewhere built of this stone include the Union Pacific station at Grand Island, Nebraska; the Bank of Italy, at Visalia, California; buildings on the campus of the University of Nevada and the University of Idaho; the Washington State College; the Ambassador apartment building in Portland; the Cathedral of St. John in Spokane; the Southern Pacific building in San Francisco; as well as in scores of others widely scattered.

The stone is available in three colors. In testing its durability for structural purposes, a cube of it two inches square was placed under a steadily increasing weight; and the stone did not crack until it had been subject to a pressure of 25,890 pounds.

Table Rock (Victor E. Thorsell Papers. Courtesy of Boise State Special Collections and Archives)

Table Rock (Courtesy of Frank Aden Jr.)

Tour 2
Boise---Arrowrock Dam---Atlanta and Return
About 150 miles

This route goes eatward out of Boise up Main Street and Warm Springs Avenue to State 21 which goes up the Boise River. The first 17 m. are oiled but thereafter the road is ordinary mountain road and sometimes fairly rough.

At 19 m. is the junction of State 21 with the Atlanta road.

Arrowrock Dam, 24 m., is the most spectacular piece of engineering in Idaho. One of the highest dams in the world, it is 353.6 feet from the river bottom, and 1,060 feet across the top. Its shape is that of the arc of a colossal cylinder jammed into the canyon, with the convex side upstream so that the body of the reservoir pushes the ends of the dam into the granite wall on either side. Steel reinforced extensions of the dam are wedged into the granite slopes of the canyon, thus solidly welding man's mountain of concrete with nature's monuments of granite. At the base the flaring toe dips 12 feet below the bed of the river and is firmly embedded in the backbone of rock.

Upon the face of the dam are twenty ports, or gates, placed in horizontal rows of ten each; and when the reservoir is filled in springtime, a few or all these are opened and the flood descends in great parabolas that spread into mist and rainbows. Each of these holes are four feet and four inches in diameter. On the floor of the river are five larger gates through which is sluiced the sediment from the bottom of the reservoir. Inside the dam is a labyrinth of tunnels and stairways and the machinery of operation. Admission is 25¢.

The reservoir is eighteen miles in length and has a storage capacity of about 300,000 acre feet, and irrigates approximately that many acres of formerly arid land. In early times it was thought that this land was worthless. During the formation of the Boise Valley, a series of volcanic craters along the northern boundary sent forth streams of lava which flowed across the valley to the southwest. Successive eruptions followed and between each there was formed a layer of soil and disintegrated rock. The upper and lower ends of the valley are now seared with deep gashes cut by the glaciers which followed the eruptions; and great moraines of sand and gravel had been left on the surface of the plain. The soil today is volcanic ash mixed with discentigrated lava, as well as the sand and gravel of the glacial moraines; and this combination has produced one of the richest soils in the West. It took water, and the construction of the Arrowrock Dam, to make the arid region blossom into what it is now.

The road to Atlanta proceeds from the dam up the river, and looks upon all sides into excellent hunting and fishing area.

Atlanta, 75 m., is a mining town in a lovely mountain basin in a primitive wilderness. It was founded in 1865 but until recently was only accessible by packtrain or by air. Though more frequently visited since this road was built up the river, it is still one of the most remote villages in the country, and one of the most interesting, because of its isolated existence, to visit. Fishing in this area is excellent.

Arrowrock Dam (Morrison-Knudsen Collection. Courtesy of Boise State Special Collections and Archives)

Atlanta, Idaho (Courtesy of the Mountain Home Historical Society)

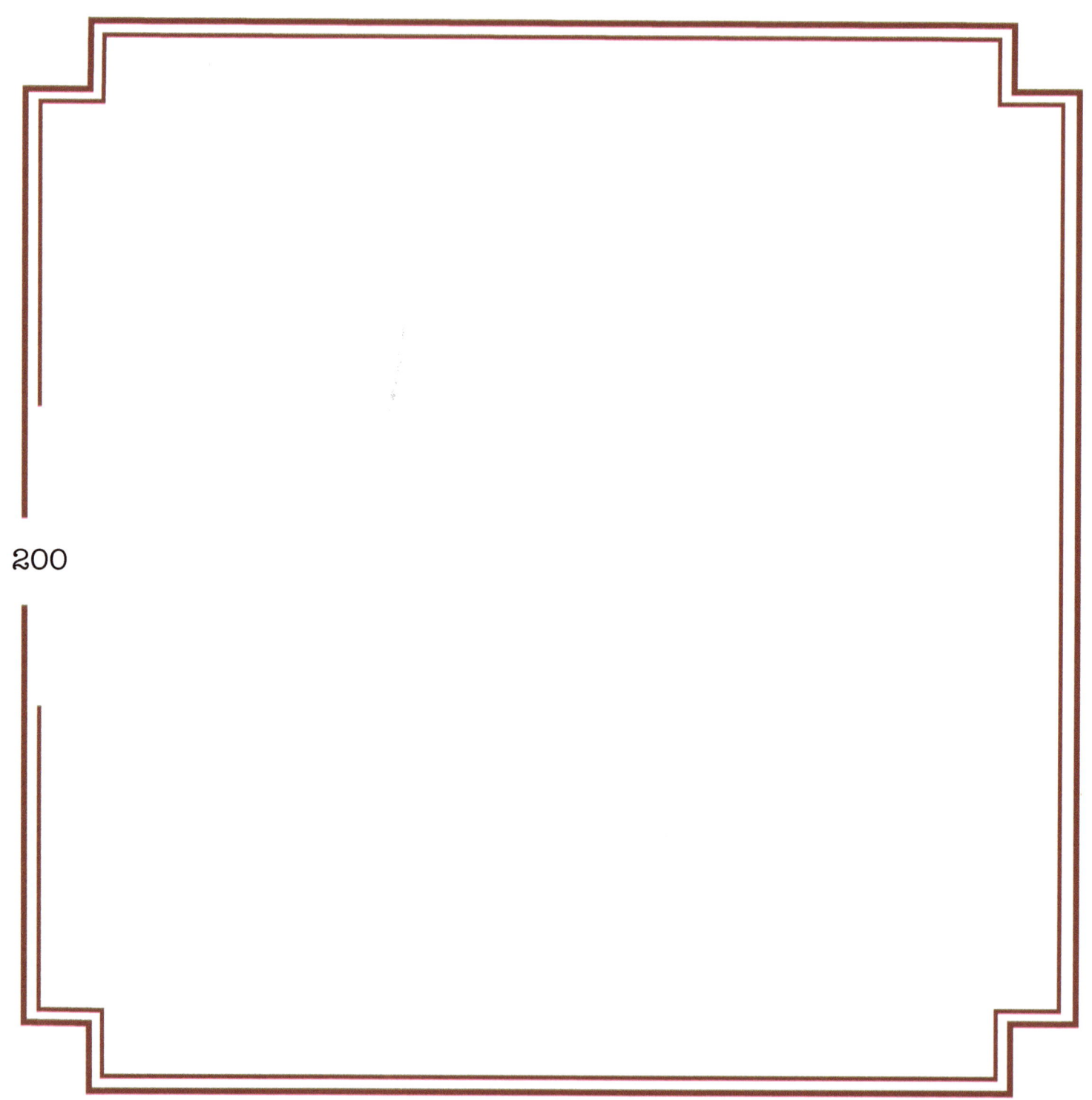

200

Acknowledgements

My thanks first to Wally Johnston and to Bruce and Laura Delaney for their support and desire to publish this manuscript. My thanks also to Brandi Burns, History Programs Manager with the City of Boise, for her initial interest in the *Boise Guide* and for introducing me to Wally and the Delaneys.

My colleagues at Albertsons Library continually offer their support and encouragement for my on-going research into Caxton Printers.

The Idaho Humanities Council and the Bibliographical Society of America provided generous grants that allowed me to travel to the Library of Congress and the National Archives.

I also wish to thank the following people and institutions for providing the images that illustrate Fisher's words: Mark Baltes of Boise; Danielle Grundel and Alisha Graefe of the Idaho State Archives; Frank E. Aden Jr. of Boise; Anne Marie Martin of Boise Public Library; Amanda Bielmann of the Boise Basque Museum & Cultural Center; Jeff Thompson of the LDS Church History Library; Beverly Schumacher and Justin Webb of Boise Music Week; Katy Shanafelt of Boise High School; Stephanie Milne-Lane of the Boise Department of Arts & History; Art Gregory of the History of Idaho Broadcasting Foundation; Jayson Petersen of Plantation Country Club; Debra Shoemaker of the Mountain Home Historical Society; Monie Hayes of the Theatre Museum of Repertoire Americana; the Library of Congress; and Boise State University Special Collections and Archives.

Alessandro Meregaglia
2019 - Boise, Idaho

www.ingramcontent.com/pod-product-compliance
Lightning Source LLC
Chambersburg PA
CBHW061142010526

44118CB00026B/2844